STREET NARCOTIC ENFORCEMENT

by
Joseph M. Klein
E. W. (Ted) Oglesby

Second Edition, June 1999
ISBN No.   0-9661369-1-8

Published by: Joe Klein Seminars
                  215 E. Orangethorpe Ave., #189
                  Fullerton, CA 92832
                  (714) 693-8897

Copies of this publication can be purchased by contacting Joe Klein Seminars.

Typesetting by Victoria Graphics, Orange, CA
Printing by KNI, Inc., Anaheim, CA

Printed in the U.S.A.

TABLE OF CONTENTS

Detective Tommy De La Rosa

<u>*DEDICATION*</u>

This book is dedicated to Detective Tommy De La Rosa of the Fullerton, California Police Department, who was killed in the line of duty June 21, 1990. Tommy was shot to death by drug dealers while working undercover. His memory and dedication to public service will never be forgotten.

ABOUT THE AUTHORS

JOSEPH M. KLEIN

Joseph M. Klein is currently a Sergeant for the Fullerton, California, Police Department, where he has served for over 24 years. As an Officer, Detective, and Supervisor, he has worked all major law enforcement assignments including Patrol, SWAT, Traffic, Investigation, Narcotics, Gangs, Drug Abuse Resistance Education (DARE), and Community Services.

During this period of time, Sergeant Klein has gained both State and National Recognition as a narcotic expert. He served four years as an Undercover Narcotic Investigator, and four years as the Supervisor of the Major Narcotic Violator Unit. He has participated in thousands of narcotic investigations, he is a Certified Drug Recognition Expert (DRE), and a court qualified drug expert. He was honored by the Orange County Narcotic Officers' Association by being selected as the *Outstanding Narcotic Supervisor of the Year*. Under his leadership, the Fullerton P.D. Narcotic Unit was awarded the *Outstanding Case of the Year Award* by the California Narcotic Officers' Association, and the *Helen Putnam Award for Excellence*, Public Safety Services, presented by the League of California Cities.

On the national level, Sergeant Klein received the *Congressional Certificate of Recognition*, for leadership in the area of narcotic enforcement, and a *Special Citation for Excellence in Narcotic Enforcement*, awarded by the U.S. Senate. He was additionally honored by the International Association of Chief's of Police, by being selected as one of the top ten police officers in the nation for his narcotic enforcement and training, and was presented with the *Public Service Award*.

While the Manager of the Department's Drug Abuse Resistance Education Program, he received the *National Program Excellence Award* from the Boys Club of America, for youth substance abuse prevention programs.

Sergeant Klein is a P.O.S.T. *Master Instructor*, and has been a teacher and law enforcement trainer for twenty years. He is currently an Instructor of Administration of Justice at Fullerton College, and he serves on the Fullerton College Academy Staff. Sergeant Klein also teaches in the Orange County Sheriff's Department's Advanced Officer Training Program, and he is an instructor for the California Narcotic Officers' Association. He is also a private substance abuse consultant and trainer, and owner of Joe Klein Seminars.

Joseph M. Klein holds a Master of Criminal Justice Degree from August Vollmer University, and a Doctor of Criminal Justice Degree from Hawthorne University.

Joe has always been active in law enforcement athletics, having won numerous state, national, and international titles in both power lifting, and track and field.

E.W. (TED) OGLESBY

E.W. (Ted) Oglesby is a Professor of Administration of Justice at Fullerton College. He served thirty-one years with the Los Angeles Police Department where he retired as a Lieutenant of Police and a Commanding Officer of one of the eighteen geographic detective divisions. During his distinguished career with LAPD, he completed fifteen different assignments, which included six years as a Detective Sergeant in the Narcotics Division where he developed extensive expertise and subsequently trained thousands of law enforcement personnel throughout California. He then taught extensively for the Drug Enforcement Administration and became a nationally recognized expert in the field of narcotics and related training for law enforcement.

Professor Oglesby is a court-qualified drug expert and has co-authored the book, *Angel Dust: What Everyone Should Know About PCP.* He has testified as a PCP expert in several highly publicized federal court cases including the infamous Rodney King trial. He has served as a spokesperson and technical advisor on drugs and law enforcement in several films and television productions.

Professor Oglesby holds a Master of Public Administration degree from the University of Southern California where he was the recipient of the coveted Pfiffner Award for the outstanding thesis of the year. Throughout his tenure with LAPD, he was very active in law enforcement athletics and was inducted into the Los Angeles Police Revolver and Athletic Club's Hall of Fame.

Professor Oglesby resides in Corona del Mar, California with his wife, Denise, who is a deputy sheriff with the Los Angeles County Sheriff's Department.

INTRODUCTION

This book is dedicated to the late Detective Tommy De La Rosa and to all of the men and women in law enforcement who have paid the ultimate price while serving and protecting the public from the dangers and violence associated with street drugs, dealers, and users. As we move into the 21st century, we are witnessing the dreadful results of extensive illicit drug use and, at the same time, we are faced with the trendy notion that drug-related incidents are merely victimless crimes and that drugs should be de-criminalized, or even legalized.

This is a powerful book written by two nationally recognized experts who have a combined total of 55 years in law enforcement and 50 years of teaching experience. They have worked the streets of southern California and have been involved in literally thousands of criminal investigations and arrests. They have provided drug training for thousands of law enforcement personnel and college students throughout their careers and continue to do so.

It is the goal of the authors to provide a guide for all readers to become more knowledgeable in the area of street drug enforcement. This book is also designed as a handbook and quick reference for law enforcement personnel and students. It is concise, accurate, easy to understand, and a valuable tool for identifying drugs and recognizing symptoms of drug abuse. As readers study this material, they will become more aware of the dangers of controlling the users and should become more conscious of personal safety issues which will, hopefully, result in fewer law enforcement deaths and injuries.

UNDER THE INFLUENCE

There are many different definitions of *under the influence*. Generally speaking, a person is considered to be under the influence anytime a chemical, natural or synthetic, is taken into the body, that causes physical or psychological impairments. This book will focus on *psychoactive drugs*. These are drugs which exert an effect in the brain.

There are many different state and federal laws that prohibit persons from using or being under the influence of certain drugs. These include alcohol, prescription drugs, illegal drugs, and in some cases over the counter drugs. There are also laws that prohibit persons from operating motor vehicles while impaired on alcohol, drugs, or a combination of both. It is suggested that the reader become familiar with the various laws that are applicable in his or her jurisdiction.

THE ADDICTION PROCESS

When drugs are introduced into the body, they eventually work their way into the bloodstream. These compounds are absorbed by the plasma (or the clear portion of the blood), and are then carried to the brain.

Once in the brain, the drug will attach to a specific group of cells called *Receptor Sites*. These receptor sites then send messages to the various parts of the body, causing *Objective Symptoms* to occur.

As long as the drug is being carried to the brain by the plasma, and the receptor site stays saturated with the drug, the subject will be under the influence. This is called the *Plasma Life*, or more commonly it is referred to as *Duration of Effects*.

The body naturally produces many different brain chemicals, referred to as *Neurochemicals* or *Neurotransmitters*. These chemicals enable us to cope with life, and to remain normal and balanced.

When the body is in need of these chemicals, they are introduced into the brain, attach to a specific receptor site, and cause certain biological reactions to occur. A classic example of this is the fight-flight response.

When faced with an immediate threat, the body releases chemicals into the brain that makes us better prepared to fight the challenge, or flee from it. These chemicals include endorphin, which is the body's natural painkiller, and norepinephrine, which is the body's natural stimulant. It is estimated that the average patrol officer experiences this fight/flight response at least four times in the course of his/her shift. (Blum, 1990)

Many of the abused substances have a similar chemical make up, as do these naturally produced Neurotransmitters. For example, an opiate has a similar structure as does endorphin, and cocaine is similar in structure to that of norepinephrine.

When a foreign compound such as heroin enters the brain, it will attach itself to the receptor site that is reserved for endorphin. After a period of time, the natural chemical is driven out of the brain. If a subject continues to ingest the drug, the body may stop producing the neurochemical all together. This is called *Negative Feedback*.

Once negative feedback occurs, the addict must now artificially saturate the receptor site with the drug to prevent the body from going into withdrawal. This is called *Biological Addiction*.

In other words, we know that the plasma life of heroin is four to six hours. That means an addict must take the drug four to six times within a 24-hour period to prevent his body from going into withdrawals.

In most cases when a person stops taking the drug, the body will eventually start producing it's own natural neurochemical again. However, in some cases the brain cells have been so damaged that the body will never again be able to repair itself. Simply put, the person is brain damaged. This is called *Post Drug Impairment Syndrome*.

WHAT IS NORMAL?

Before we can determine if a person is under the influence, we must first understand what is "normal."

The *Under the Influence* evaluation is merely a series of observations. The evaluating officer is looking for a combination of objective symptoms that are consistent with the intoxicating effects of one or more drugs.

A determination of drug influence should not be made based solely on one or two observations, but rather on the totality of the examination.

PUPIL RANGE

The pupil is the dark colored center portion of the eye. It is actually a hole in the iris (the colored part of the eye) which is a muscle that dilates and constricts. The medical term for a constricted pupil is miosis, and the medical term for a dilated pupil is mydriasis.

The normal pupil will constrict to 3.0 mm and dilate to 6.5 mm. Many things can cause the pupil to dilate and constrict, these include:

- *Light* - When light is applied to the eye, the pupils will constrict. When light is reduced, the pupil will dilate. It should only take the normal pupil one second to react to the absence or presence of light.

- *Drugs* - This may include illegal drugs, prescription drugs, alcohol, and over the counter drugs.

- *Injuries or Diseases* – Those conditions that specifically impact the central nervous system, or the eye, may have an effect on the pupil. For example, medication for glaucoma may cause the pupil to constrict, tertiary syphilis will usually cause only one pupil to constrict, and a blow to the head may cause one pupil to dilate (usually on the opposite side of the injury).

- *Natural or Congenital* - The person may have been born with large or small pupils. Also, during the *fight/flight* response, the pupils will dilate, but only for a few seconds.

There is **no** medical evidence to establish that pupil size varies depending on the eye color. However, the pupil size of persons with light colored eyes may appear larger than people with dark colored eyes, for it is easier to see.

There **is** medical evidence to support the fact that very young people, and very old people, may naturally have constricted pupils. In young people, the central nervous system has not yet fully developed, and in older people, the central nervous system has started to break down. Both of these conditions may affect the pupil size.

Many field officers, especially those working DARE (Drug Abuse Resistance Education) and School Resource assignments, report seeing dilated pupils on adolescents. This may be due to chemical and hormonal changes that naturally occur during puberty and adolescence. Yet officers need to be aware that substance abuse among our youth has increased dramatically over recent years.

OTHER CONDITIONS OF THE EYE

- *Nystagmus* - This is the distinct jerky movements of the eyeball both horizontally and vertically. Nystagmus can be caused by impairments to the central nervous system, eye, and inner ear. It can also be caused by natural or congenital conditions, or by drug and alcohol intoxication. Depressants (including alcohol), inhalants, and PCP will most likely cause horizontal nystagmus. These same drugs taken in high doses will usually cause vertical nystagmus.

- *Non-Convergence (Lack of Convergence)* - This is the inability of the eyes to cross and stay crossed. Alcohol, depressants, inhalants, PCP, and cannabis may cause this condition.

- *Hippus* - This is the pulsating of the pupil within a .5mm range. This may be caused by drug intoxication (usually stimulants), poly-drug use (stimulants mixed with narcotic analgesics), or withdrawal from heroin.

- *Rebound Dilation* - This is when a dilated pupil constricts with the application of light, then with the light still applied, it dilates in a pulsating fashion, often times back to the original size. This is often caused by marijuana intoxication.

- *Reddened Sclera* - The sclera is the white part of the eyeball. This is commonly known as blood shot eyes.

OTHER VITAL SIGNS

- *Pulse* - The average pulse range is between 60 to 90 beats per minute.

- *Blood Pressure* - The blood pressure is the force exerted by the blood against the walls of the blood vessels. The top number is the systolic pressure, which measures the pressure as the heart pumps or constricts. This bottom number is the diastolic pressure, which measures the pressure while the heart is at rest. The average blood pressure is between 120/70 to 140/90.

- *Respiration* - The average person takes in approximately 20 breaths per minute.

- *Body Temperature* - The normal body temperature is 98.6 degrees.

- *Romberg Exam* - Most people have the ability to estimate a time period of thirty seconds, within an accuracy of a few seconds. This is also called the internal time clock test. Persons who estimate thirty seconds when actually more time has elapsed (ie.) 50 seconds are said to have a delayed Romberg. People who estimate thirty seconds when actually less time has elapsed (i.e. 10 seconds) are said to have a rapid Romberg. Stimulants will usually cause a rapid Romberg, and narcotic analgesics and depressants will usually cause a delayed Romberg. Other drugs such as hallucinogens and marijuana may cause a distorted Romberg.

Under the influence exam.

UNDER THE INFLUENCE EVALUATIONS

The *Under The Influence* evaluation is simply a series of observations. The evaluating officer notes the objective symptoms being displayed, and compares them against what he/she knows to be "normal." These authors recommend that whenever possible, all observations and opinions be made while in the field prior to the arrest. It is also recommended that if the suspect is arrested, a secondary evaluation be conducted in the station or jail. The reason being that during the in custody evaluation, lighting and other conditions can be controlled.

There are several recognized protocols for conducting the under the influence evaluation. Most of these include the following observations.

THE PROFILE

Note the subject's general demeanor and appearance. Describe what the subject looks like, what he is doing, and how he is acting. Note if the subject is rational; note his cognitive abilities, speech, balance, and behavior. Note if the subject is in touch with reality, and if he can comprehend or respond to your questions.

Based on the subject's demeanor and outward appearance, you should start to form an opinion as to what the subject is under the influence of. For example: If a subject is looking sedated and lethargic, has slow and slurred speech, droopy eyelids, is scratching his face and neck, and has dried lips, you should suspect heroin influence.

If a subject is hyperactive, talking rapidly, constantly fidgeting, breathing rapidly, has an overheated appearance, is overreacting to the situation, or acting agitated or paranoid, it is likely the subject is under the influence of cocaine or methamphetamine.

If a subject is standing naked in the middle of the street,

will not respond to your commands, has a blank stare on his face, and appears to be hallucinating, there is a good chance that he is loaded on PCP or some other type of hallucinogenic drug.

This is the most important step, for it lays the foundation for your probable cause to detain and conduct further evaluations.

THE EYE EXAMINATION

- *Pupils* - First look at the pupils, and note if they appear to be dilated or constricted. Now with the use of a pupilometer, measure both pupils, and determine if they are within the normal range. In bright light the pupil should be around 3.0 mm. In room light, most pupils are approximately 4.5 mm. In dark light, the pupils should be dilated up to 6.5 mm.

- *Reaction to Light* - With the use of a low beam flashlight apply light directly into each eye for a period of approximately 15 seconds. Note if the pupil constricts, and stays constricted. If it takes longer than one second for the pupil to constrict, this is considered a slow reaction. When the light is removed, the pupil should dilate back to the normal pupil range, considering the existing lighting conditions. Also look for hippus, rebound dilation, and reddened sclera.

If you are conducting the evaluation in bright light, you may not be able to see much pupillary response. If this is the case, have the subject close his eyes and cover them with his hands. Have him hold this position for at least one minute. Hold your pupilometer next to the subject's face, have him open his eyes, and quickly measure the pupils. The normal pupil will be dilated, then quickly constrict.

- *Nystagmus* - Hold your finger, or some other stimuli, in a vertical position, at a distance of about 12 to 15 inches, directly in front of the person's nose. Have the subject keep his head straight, and with his eyes track your finger as you slowly move it to both sides of the head. Also have him track your finger as you move it up and down. Note the ability of the eyes to track smoothly, and look for distinct jerking at maximum deviation, noting the angle of onset.

- *Non-Convergence* - Also check for convergence by bringing your finger to the tip of the subject's nose. Many different drugs disable the ability of the eyes to converge, and one eye may drift away from your fingertip. This is also called lack of convergence or strabismus.

VITAL SIGNS

- *Pulse* - Take the subject's pulse, and calculate how many times the heart beats in one minute. Most protocols recommend that you take the subject's pulse three times during the course of the evaluation.

- *Blood Pressure* – If possible take the subject's blood pressure.

- *Respiration* - Count how many times the person's chest or stomach rises or falls in one minute.

- *Body Temperature* - Feel if the subject is warm, or cold and clammy. Note if he/she is sweating. If possible, take the subject's temperature with the use of a thermometer.

The evaluating officer can personally obtain these vital signs him/herself, or medical personnel can provide them.

THE ROMBERG EXAMINATION

Have the subject stand in a modified position of attention, eyes closed, and head tilting backward. Have the subject estimate when he/she thinks that 30 seconds has passed. Also note if the subject is swaying, fidgeting, grinding his teeth, or displaying eyelid tremors.

SIGNS OF INGESTION

*   *Injection Sites* - Start by looking for injection marks on the arms, hands, or neck. Addicts have been known to inject on every part of the body including the genital area, the legs, or under the tongue.

    Remember if you ask a suspect to roll up his sleeves or take off his jacket, it could constitute a search, so make sure you follow the proper rules of evidence.

    For the purpose of the under the influence evaluation, we are primarily concerned with fresh injection sites. These are characteristic of small puncture wounds, usually directly over a blood vessel, which are red, raised, with the presence of body fluids still visible.

    The evaluating officer should note and describe all old puncture wounds that are in various stages of healing, and other scar tissue caused by substance abuse. This is good evidence to establish a pattern or history of addiction.

*   *Nose* - You might see residue running out of the nose, but most often you will have to examine the nasal passages. Have the subject tilt his head back, shine a flashlight up each nostril and look for powder attached to the nose hairs. Also note any sores or irritation that could have been caused by substance abuse.

- *Odors* – Note any odors on the person's breath or person.

- *Burns* - Check for burn marks on the subject's hands and face.

- *Residue* - Check for residue inside the subject's mouth, on his person, and on items in his possession.

DRUGS AND PARAPHERNALIA

Identify any drugs or drug paraphernalia in the subject's possession. This includes use paraphernalia, cuts, and packaging material.

FIELD INTERVIEW

Every objective symptom of drug influence can also be caused by medical disorders, injuries, or congenital conditions. Before it can be determined that a subject is under the influence of a controlled substance all of the above legitimate explanations must be eliminated. To do this, ask the subject:

- Are you injured or sick?
- Are you being treated by a doctor or dentist?
- Are you taking any medications?
- Have you been drinking alcohol?
- Do you have any head injuries?
- Do you have any eye injuries or problems?
- Are you applying any medication to your eyes?
- Do you have, or are you being treated for Glaucoma?
- Do you have, or are you being treated for Syphilis?
- Do you have any problems with your heart or blood pressure?
- Do you have any respiratory problems?
- When did you last eat?
- When did you last sleep?

If the subject answers "yes" to any of the above, have him be specific as to the exact condition, how the injury or sickness was caused, type of treatment he is receiving, how long he has been treated, the name of the doctor who is treating him, and the type and dosage of medication being taken.

Ask the subject questions to establish his/her cognitive skills. Such question should include:

- Do you know where you are?
- Do you know what day it is?
- Do you know what time it is?

Ask the suspect questions about his drug use and history. These questions should include:

- Are you currently using drugs?
- When did you last use?
- What type of drugs did you use?
- How much did you use?
- How did you use it?
- Where were you when you last used?
- How do you feel now?
- Are you on probation or parole?

Make sure that these questions are asked while in the field, prior to placing the suspect under arrest. Once the suspect is in custody, all questions should be obtained in compliance with the Miranda decision.

CHEMICAL TEST

In order to convict a person of being under the influence of drugs, most jurisdictions require a chemical test. Most controlled substances can be detected in both the blood and urine, but it is important to remember that most compounds will not reach the urine for at least one hour after use.

THE "DRE" PROCESS

The DRE (Drug Recognition Expert) Drug Evaluation and Classification Program has long been recognized as a validated, systematic method for determining drug related impairments.

The DRE program classifies drugs as follows:

- *Central Nervous System Depressants*
- *Inhalants*
- *PCP*
- *Cannabis*
- *Central Nervous System Stimulants*
- *Hallucinogens*
- *Narcotic Analgesics*

The DRE examination is best suited for the in custody evaluation. The following is the 12-step process.

1. BREATH ALCOHOL SCREENING TEST

The evaluating officer first obtains a breath alcohol screen to determine the presence of alcohol and the blood alcohol content.

Once obtaining this information, the evaluator can make a determination if the observable impairments are consistent with alcohol intoxication.

2. INTERVIEW OF ARRESTING OFFICER

If the evaluating officer did not conduct the field investigation, the arresting officer is interviewed as to the circumstances of the arrest, and impairments or symptomatology observed in the field.

3. PRELIMINARY EXAMINATION

The evaluator conducts a preliminary examination to rule out any obvious medical conditions. This examination includes taking of the pulse, a check for horizontal nystagmus and angle of onset, and an initial estimation of the pupil size. The evaluating officer also interviews the suspect as to his medical condition, and use of drugs. Questions are also asked to evaluate the suspect's cognitive skills.

4. EYE EXAM

This includes determining the size of both pupils, checking for horizontal gaze nystagmus (smooth pursuit, maximum deviation, and angle of onset), vertical nystagmus, and non-convergence.

5. DIVIDED ATTENTION TESTS

This is also referred to as the Standardized Field Sobriety Test. Four tests are administered during this phase.

- *Romberg* (30 second internal time clock, body sway)

- *Walk and Turn* (walking a straight line, heel to toe, nine steps in each direction)

- *One Leg Stance* (left leg then right leg, 30 seconds each leg)

- *Finger to Nose* (left/right, left/right, right/left)

6. VITAL SIGNS

The evaluator determines the blood pressure, body temperature, and obtains a second pulse rate.

7. DARK ROOM

This includes four separate examinations of the pupil.
- *Room light*
- *Near total darkness*
- *Indirect light*
- *Direct light*

Also during this step, the oral and nasal cavities are examined for residue.

8. CHECK FOR MUSCLE TONE

The muscle tone is checked to determine if it is rigid, flaccid, or normal.

9. CHECK FOR INJECTION SITES AND THIRD PULSE

The officer conducts an examination for injection sites, and obtains the third and final pulse rate.

10. INTERROGATION, STATEMENTS, AND OTHER OBSERVATIONS

The officer notes any statements made by the suspect during the course of the evaluation, conducts an in custody interview, and includes any other observations regarding the suspect's drug impairments.

11. OPINION OF THE EVALUATOR

The evaluator gives an opinion as to what drug category he/she believes the subject to be under the influence of.

12. TOXICOLOGICAL EXAMINATION

NARCOTIC ANALGESICS

BACKGROUND

There are three sources of Narcotic Analgesics, sometimes referred to as opioids, or narcotics. The first source is derived from the Opium Poppy (Papaver Somniferum L.). The plant is grown throughout the world, primarily in the Far East, the Middle East, Asia, Southeast Asia, Mexico and South America. This includes the natural opium alkaloids such as Morphine, Codeine and Thebaine. It also includes opium derivatives such as Heroin, Dilaudid, Hycodan, Percodan, and Metopon.

The second source is synthetically manufactured. This includes many legitimate prescription drugs such as Demerol, Methadone, Numorphan, Fentanyl, and Darvon.

The third source is found in the human body. The brain and adrenal glands produce a chemical called endorphin; this is the body's natural painkiller. Endorphin also helps control stress and maintain mental stability.

Heroin (Diacetylmorphine) is the most widely abused of all the opiates. The reason being, heroin is very water-soluble and causes the least amount of trauma to the skin tissue when injected. Heroin also stays active in the body longer than most other opiates.

The conversion of heroin from opium is a relatively simple process. The raw opium is heated and dissolved in water. Lime or lime based fertilizer is added, then the solution is filtered. Concentrated ammonia is then added, causing morphine crystals to solidify. The solution is filtered again to isolate the morphine, then the substance is heated again and acetyl anhydride is added producing heroin.

Opium Poppy

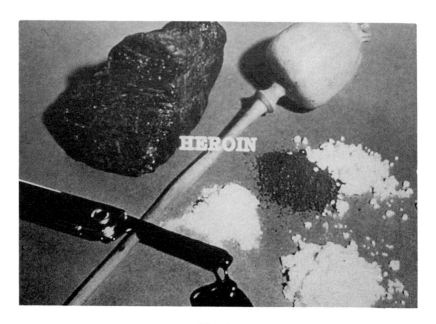

Heroin

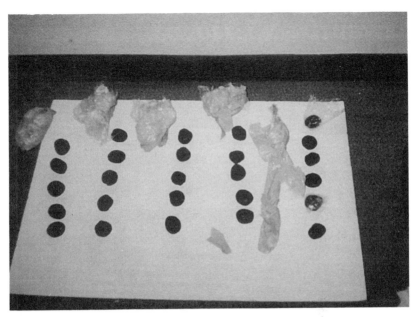

Black Tar Heroin

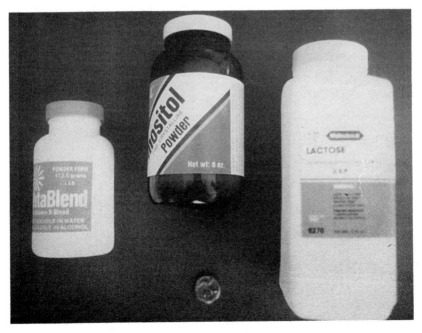

Cutting Agents

RECOGNITION

- *China White* - This is a white powder, usually produced in Asia or Europe, and smuggled into the United States by the Italian Mafia, and other criminal organizations. With the large influx of immigration into California from Southeast Asia, China White is an emerging West Coast problem. Southeast Asian street gangs have expanded their criminal endeavors into the distribution of this drug.

- *Black Tar* - This is a crude form of heroin produced in Mexico, in what are referred to as kitchen labs. This term is used due to the fact that kitchen implements are used in the conversion process. This is a black sap like substance resembling common tar.

- *Mexican Brown* - This is a brown or off-white in color, powdered substance. It is produced in the same fashion as is black tar heroin. However, when making Mexican Brown, the tar is processed one step further to turn it into a powder.

- *Smoking Heroin (Opium)* - This has an appearance similar to black tar heroin. Opium has been smoked in some Asian cultures for centuries. Again, with the influx of Asian immigrants into the United States, the smoking of opium has been seen with frequency in the Asian community.

Colombia has also recently emerged as a major producer of smoking heroin. The smoking of heroin has also become popular within the young coffee shop and nightclub circles.

METHODS OF INGESTION

- Smoked (Chasing the Dragon)
- Snorted

- Injected
- Orally

STREET SLANG

- Shit
- Gow
- Goma
- Pura
- Brown

- Chiva
- Tar
- Stuff
- Negro
- Black

METHODS OF PACKAGING

- Balloons
- Bindles
- Cellophane

SYMPTOMATOLOGY (OVERVIEW)

Heroin is the most widely abused narcotic analgesic. Heroin, like the other narcotic analgesics, depresses the functions of the central nervous system and it is a very powerful painkiller. Upon entering the body, heroin is metabolized into morphine within 2 to 3 minutes. Morphine very closely resembles the neurotransmitter endorphin, which is the body's natural painkiller. Once in the brain, the morphine attaches to the receptor sites previously reserved for endorphin, sending out impulses or messages that cause the objective symptoms of opiate influence.

EYES

- *Constricted Pupils* - Heroin will constrict the pupils under 3.0 millimeters. It only takes about 4-6 mgs. of heroin (1000 mgs. equals 1 gram) to constrict the pupil. Pupillary constriction will occur approximately 10 to 15 minutes after use. In chronic users, the other outward objective symptoms may not be noticeable, but the pupils will still be constricted.

- *Reaction to Light* - Heroin will keep the pupils constricted and non-reactive to light for approximately four to six hours, depending on the dosage taken, and the tolerance of the user.

- *Reddened Sclera* - Heroin will often cause the eyes to be bloodshot.

- *Other Conditions* - Heroin will *not* cause nystagmus, lack of convergence, hippus, or rebound dilation.

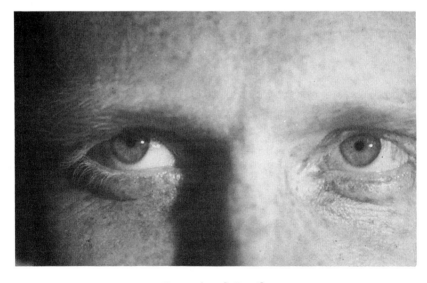

Constricted Pupils

DEPRESSION OF THE CENTRAL NERVOUS SYSTEM

Heroin will depress the functions of the central nervous system, and will impair motor coordination. A person under the influence of heroin may have:

- *Reduced Pulse Rate* - under 60 beats per minute.
- *Lowered Respiration Rate* - under 20 per minute.
- *Reduced Blood Pressure* - under 120/70.
- *Low Body Temperature* - under 98.6 degrees.

ROMBERG EXAM

A person under the influence of a narcotic analgesic will have a delayed Romberg.

EUPHORIA

Depending on how the drug is ingested, an euphoric feeling or "rush" will come on within a few minutes and peak in about 15 minutes. This will be followed by a feeling of well being and sedation.

DRY MOUTH

Heroin will constrict the flow of many body fluids, so it is common for someone under the influence to:

- be licking his lips
- complain of thirst
- have dry and cracked lips
- have dried saliva caked on the lips

SCRATCHING

It is common for someone who is under the influence of heroin to scratch their face, neck, and arms. This is thought to be caused by the stimulation of the nerve endings near the surface of the skin. Heroin use also releases histamines into the body, which also causes scratching and irritation.

OTHER SYMPTOMS

- Lethargy
- The person may appear to fall asleep, or "Nod Off."
- Relaxed facial muscles
- Droopy eyelids
- Slow and deliberate speech
- Slow or deliberate walk
- Cold or clammy skin

SIGNS OF INGESTION

An addict will inject himself in any blood vessel (intravenous), starting with the most convenient location. They will usually start with the inner elbow area, then move to the back of the hands, forearms, triceps area, neck, legs, feet, breasts, or the genital area.

Repeated unsanitary injections traumatize the skin, causing a tattooing effect and a build-up of scar tissue. This condition is commonly known as "tracks." Tracks will usually be hardened areas of scar tissue, with discolored skin, over blood vessels. It is estimated that one inch of scar tissue represents between 100 to 150 injection sites.

A fresh injection wound is one that is red and raised with the presence of body fluids. A puncture wound caused by an illegal, unsanitary injection may bleed or ooze body fluids for up to 24 hours.

Most addicts have numerous puncture wounds in various stages of healing. Depending on the user's health and hygiene, a puncture wound scab will be visible for about two weeks.

Some users will inject into the muscle tissue (*intramuscu-*

lar), and others will inject under the skin *(subcutaneous)*. This is also referred to as *skin popping*.

DURATION OF EFFECTS

The plasma life of heroin is four to six hours, so the addict must inject himself 4 to 6 times per day. It takes approximately 1 to 2 hours for the heroin to reach the urine, but it can be detected 48 to 72 hours after use.

WITHDRAWAL

Persons who are *biologically addicted* to heroin will begin to experience withdrawal symptoms four to six hours after the last use. They will suffer:

- Insomnia
- Muscle and joint pain
- Nausea
- Chills
- Diaphoresis (sweating)
- Piloerection (gooseflesh)
- Hyperactive reflexes (jerking)
- Yawning
- Lacrimation (tearing)
- Rhinorrhea (runny nose)
- Vomiting
- Diarrhea
- Dilated pupils over 6.5 mm
- Tachycardia (rapid pulse)

Withdrawal symptoms may last for several weeks. It is important to note that subjects experiencing withdrawal symptoms **are not** under the influence for prosecution purposes.

SUMMARY

Horizontal Gaze Nystagmus	*No*
Vertical Gaze Nystagmus	*No*
Non-Convergence	*No*
Pupil Size	*Constricted*
Pupillary Reaction to Light	*Little or None*
Pulse Rate	*Down*
Blood Pressure	*Down*
Body Temperature	*Down*
Muscle Tone	*Flaccid*
Romberg Exam	*Slow*

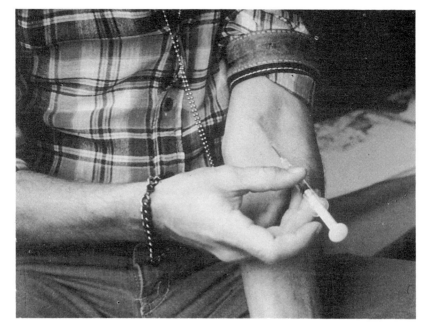

Suspect injecting heroin

COCAINE

BACKGROUND

Cocaine (Benzoylmethylecgonine) is an alkaloid of the Coca Plant (Erythroxylon Coca) which is grown primarily in South America. Cocaine has a legitimate medical use as a topical anesthetic, and is commonly used in oral, nasal, and optic surgery.

To produce one kilogram of cocaine, approximately 100 kilograms of coca leafs are harvested and dried. The leaves are then treated in a chemical process, which includes the addition of a strong alkali such as lime, petroleum products, and sulfuric acid. The result is coca paste. The paste is then treated with hydrochloric acid, producing *cocaine hydrochloride*.

RECOGNITION

* *Cocaine Hydrochloride* - This is the powdered form of cocaine. It is usually white, off-white, or yellowish in color. When packaged in kilogram quantities, the powder is compressed into bricks. The cocaine may appear in a rock-like form, but is not to be confused with *"rock cocaine."*

* *Cocaine Base* - This is cocaine that has been freebased into a solid form. This process is very simple. Cocaine Hydrochloride is mixed with water and baking soda. When the substance is heated the cut or impurities separate, leaving cocaine base. The rock that is left dries into a hard solid form, and is also white or off-white in color. Cocaine base is often referred to as Rock, Crack, Base, or Freebase.

Cocaine

Cocaine

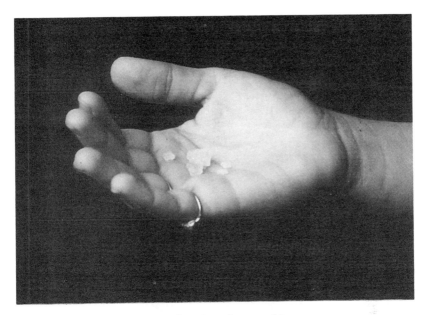

Cocaine (crack or rock)

METHODS OF INGESTION

- Snorted
- Smoked
- Injected
- Orally

Cocaine Hydrochloride (powdered cocaine) can be absorbed into the body usually by snorting it into the nose, smoking, or by injecting it into a blood vessel. Some people take the drug orally by mixing it with coffee or other beverages, or by putting it in gelatin capsules and swallowing them.

Rock or free-based cocaine is smoked. The substance does not burn like tobacco, rather it vaporizes, and these vapors are inhaled.

STREET SLANG

- Coke
- White
- Blow
- Snow
- Flake
- Cola
- Toot
- Blanco

METHODS OF PACKAGING

- Paper Bindles
- Glass Vials
- Balloons
- Cellophane Baggies
- Kilograms – Pressed into rectangle bricks, wrapped with duct tape or other packaging tape, often with various types of markings on the exterior.

SYMPTOMATOLOGY (OVERVIEW)

Cocaine is a very powerful central nervous system stimulant, and biological addiction develops very rapidly. Upon entering the bloodstream, cocaine is metabolized into *benzoylecgonine*. Cocaine has a similar chemical make up as the neurotransmitter norepinephrine, which is the body's natural stimulant.

EYES

- *Dilated Pupils* – When a person is under the influence of cocaine, the pupils will dilate over 6.5 mm. It is not unusual to find pupils dilated to 10.0 mm. It should be noted that some police officers have reported that in chronic cocaine users, the drug actually causes the pupil to constrict.

- *Slow Reaction to Light* – The pupils of persons under the influence of cocaine will react slowly to the absence and presence of light.

- *Hippus* - Upon applying light into the eyes, the pupils will pulsate (dilate and constrict) usually within a .5 mm. range.

- *Rebound Dilation* - Often times when light is applied directly into the eye, the pupil may slowly constrict then re-dilate.

- *Reddened Sclera* - Cocaine use will often cause the eyes to appear bloodshot and glassy. This is caused by the user going long periods of time without sleep.

- *Other Conditions* - Cocaine will not cause nystagmus, or non-convergence.

STIMULATION OF THE CENTRAL NERVOUS SYSTEM

- Elevated Pulse - Cocaine may elevate the pulse over 90 beats per minute. It is not unusual for cocaine to increase the pulse rate as high as 180 beats per minute.

- *Elevated Blood Pressure* - Cocaine will elevate the blood pressure over 140/90.

- *Increased Respiration* - A person under the influence of cocaine may have a respiration rate of over 20 breaths per minute.

- *Elevated Body Temperature* - over 98.6 degrees.

ROMBERG EXAM

A person under the influence of cocaine will display a rapid Romberg. While performing this test, the user may display eyelid tremors, bruxism and fidgeting.

HYPERACTIVITY

A person under the influence of cocaine will be hyperactive, agitated, or "wired." Such behavior could include:

- Excitability
- Rapid speech
- Sweating
- Paranoia
- Agitation
- Aggressive or assaultive behavior

EUPHORIA

When cocaine is ingested into the body, a "rush" or "high" will come on within 5 minutes, and last for about 15 minutes. If the drug is injected or smoked, the "high" is said to come on quicker and be more intense. As a general rule, the quicker the onset of intoxication, the shorter the duration of effects.

LETHARGY

If cocaine is taken in very high doses, a person may display the outward symptoms of lethargy, staggering, slurred speech, and may appear drunk. People in this condition are in a pre-overdose state, and need immediate medical attention.

HALLUCINATIONS

Cocaine taken in high doses may cause hallucinations. This is often referred to as *cocaine psychosis*. People in this condition are usually in a highly disorientated, paranoid and delusional state. People in this condition can be very dangerous.

OTHER SYMPTOMS

- Severe depression
- Paranoia
- Insomnia
- Loss of appetite
- Radical mood swings
- Impaired motor functions
- Impaired cognitive abilities
- Grinding of the teeth (Bruxism)
- Distortion of time
- Tremors
- Convulsions
- Coma
- Death

SIGNS OF INGESTION

When cocaine is snorted into the nose, one might observe irritation around, or inside of the nasal passages. Often times cocaine residue can be seen inside of the nostrils, or dripping out of the nose.

If a user injects the drug, puncture wounds may be present over the blood vessels. Cocaine seems to cause a great deal of trauma to the skin tissue. This is evident by bruising of the skin around injection sites, abscessing and infection.

If a person smokes "crack" or "freebase" cocaine, it is not unusual to see burn marks on the lips, inside of the mouth, face, and hands.

DURATION OF EFFECTS

Depending on the method of ingestion, the rush or euphoric effect of cocaine lasts 5 to 15 minutes, however the plasma life of cocaine is three to six hours.

The body metabolizes cocaine into benzoylecgonine in about one hour after use. This is about the same amount of time that the noticeable objective symptoms start to diminish. Benzoylecgonine can be detected in the urine for as long as 48 hours after use.

WITHDRAWAL SYMPTOMS

A person who is biologically addicted to cocaine will start to experience withdrawal symptoms three to six hours after use. This is characteristic by:

* Severe depression
* Paranoia
* Irritability
* Lethargy
* Mental confusion
* Memory loss
* Suicide

SUMMARY

Horizontal Gaze Nystagmus	No
Vertical Gaze Nystagmus	No
Non-Convergence	No
Pupil Size	Dilated
Pupillary Reaction to Light	Slow
Pulse Rate	Up
Blood Pressure	Up
Body Temperature	Up
Muscle Tone	Rigid
Romberg Exam	Fast

AMPHETAMINES

BACKGROUND

Amphetamine is a synthetic stimulant, first synthesized in 1927 for medical purposes. This drug continues to have legitimate medical uses including the treatment of narcolepsy, the control of hyperactivity in children, the relief of fatigue, treatment for depression, appetite control, and the treatment of Parkinson's Disease. Some of these legitimate pharmaceutical medications include Dexedrine, Benzedrine, Biphetamine, and Desoxyn.

There are also non-amphetamine stimulants, which are prescribed for medical purposes including Ritalin, Preludin, and Cylert. These medications can also be abused.

Methamphetamine, sometimes referred to as methadrine, is the most widely abused of all amphetamines. It is available under the trade name of Desoxyn, yet most methamphetamine abused on the streets is illegally produced in clandestine laboratories. California has emerged as a major source for the underground production of this drug.

There are many different methods for the clandestine production of methamphetamine. The two most common methods are the P-2-P method, and the Ephedrine method.

The P-2-P method is also known as "biker meth" because of the heavy involvement of the outlaw motorcycle gangs in its production and distribution. In this method, phenyl-2-propanone (P-2-P) is the primary precursor.

The ephedrine method is sometimes called "Mexican meth" because of the heavy involvement of Mexican Nationals in its production and distribution. In this method ephedrine is used as the primary precursor. As much as 80% of all methamphetamine seized in California is ephedrine based.

The following is a list of common precursors (chemicals) commonly found in methamphetamine labs.

- Phenyl-2-Propanone (P-2-P)
- Ephedrine
- Freon
- Ether
- Methylamine
- Lye
- Hydriodic Acid
- Red Phosphorus
- Hydrochloric Acid
- Iodine Crystals
- Sulfuric Acid
- Hydrogen Gas
- Sodium Hydroxide
- Sodium Cyanide
- Acetone

__RECOGNITION__

- *Methamphetamine Hydrochloride* - This is most often seen in a powdered form, usually white, off-white, yellow, or brown in color. It can also be found in a solid crystal form, or even in a brown paste form similar in appearance to peanut butter. One narcotic enforcement officer reports seeing it in a black gum like appearance, similar to that of black tar heroin.

- *Ice (d-methamphetamine hydrochloride)* - This is the freebase form of Methamphetamine. Ice looks like crystal rocks; it is clear or translucent, and similar in appearance to rock candy. Like crack cocaine, *Ice* methamphetamine is smoked.

Ice, primarily manufactured in Korea, first appeared in Hawaii in the 1980's. The "high" is said to be more intense than powered methamphetamine, and reportedly lasts much longer. Ice has been seen on the streets of Western United States, but not with the frequency originally predicted.

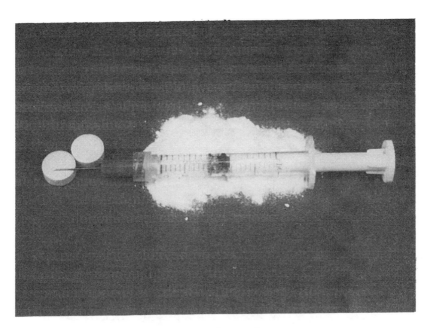

Methamphetamine

Methamphetamine (Ice)

49

Methamphetamine

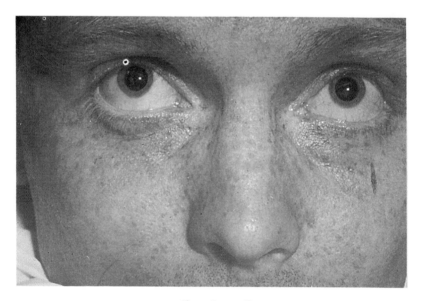

Dilated Pupils

METHODS OF INGESTION

- Injected
- Snorted
- Smoked
- Orally

STREET SLANG

- Meth
- Speed
- Crystal
- Ice
- Crystal Meth

- Go Fast
- Crank
- Glass
- Tweek
- Uppers

METHODS OF PACKAGING

- Paper bindles
- Glass vials
- Cellophane baggies

SYMPTOMATOLOGY (OVERVIEW)

Methamphetamine is a very powerful synthetically produced central nervous system stimulant. It is believed that the chemical make up of methamphetamine closely resembles the neurochemical serotonin. Serotonin plays an important role in maintaining stable moods and emotions, and it helps regulate the sleep cycle.

Methamphetamine also interacts with other neurochemicals including dopamine, epinephrine and norepinephrine. Dopamine is closely associated with the body's pleasure response, and epinephrine and norepinephrine are both naturally produced stimulants.

The objective symptoms of methamphetamine influence are the same as cocaine.

EYES

- *Dilated Pupils* - When a person is under the influence of methamphetamine, the pupils will dilate over 6.5 mm. and can be as large as 10.0 mm. Like with cocaine, it has been reported that in chronic methamphetamine users, the pupil may constrict.

- *Slow Reaction to Light* - The pupils of persons under the influence of methamphetamine will react slowly to the absence and presence of light.

- *Rebound Dilation* - This condition may be present with methamphetamine influence.

- *Hippus* - This condition may also be present with methamphetamine influence.

- *Reddened Sclera* - Since persons under the influence of methamphetamine may go long periods of time without sleep; the eyes may appear bloodshot and glassy.

- *Other Conditions* - Methamphetamine will not cause nystagmus, or non-convergence.

STIMULATION OF THE CENTRAL NERVOUS SYSTEM

- *Elevated Pulse* - Methamphetamine may elevate the pulse over 90 beats per minute.

- *Elevated Blood Pressure* - Methamphetamine will elevate the blood pressure over 140/90.

- *Increased Respiration* - A person under the influence of methamphetamine may have a respiration rate of over 20 breaths per minute.

- *High Body Temperature* - over 98.6 degrees.

ROMBERG EXAM

A person under the influence of methamphetamine may display a rapid Romberg. Also look for eyelid tremors, bruxism, and fidgeting.

HYPERACTIVITY

A person under the influence of methamphetamine may display hyperactive behavior such as:

- Excitability
- Rapid speech
- Paranoia
- Agitation
- Aggressive or assaultive behavior

EUPHORIA

Like cocaine, methamphetamine will cause an initial intense "rush" or "high," that will come on within 5 minutes, and last for about 15 minutes. The person will continue to feel "wired" for several hours after use.

LETHARGY

If taken in very high doses, methamphetamine may cause outward symptoms of lethargy, staggering, slurred speech, and a drunkenness appearance.

HALLUCINATIONS

Methamphetamine can also cause hallucinations. These hallucinations are often associated with fear, paranoia, and aggression.

OTHER SYMPTOMS

- Sweating
- Severe depression
- Paranoia
- Insomnia
- Loss of appetite
- Radical mood swings
- Impaired motor functions
- Impaired cognitive abilities
- Grinding of the teeth (Bruxism)
- Distortion of time
- Tremors
- Convulsions
- Coma
- Death

SIGNS OF INGESTION

If a person snorts methamphetamine, it may cause irritation and bleeding of the nose. One might see residue inside of the nose, or dripping out of the nostrils.

If a person injects methamphetamine, puncture wounds can be noticed over the blood vessels. Methamphetamine often causes a great deal of trauma and damage to the skin tissue, characteristic by bruising, reddening, and swelling around the injection site. These wounds are often called "speed bumps."

If a person smokes "ice," or methamphetamine in the powder form, it is not unusual to see burn marks on the lips, inside of the mouth, on the face, and hands.

DURATION OF EFFECTS

The length of time that methamphetamine will stay active in the plasma is between 4 to 8 hours. It can be detected in the urine one hour after use, and up to 48 hours after use.

WITHDRAWAL SYMPTOMS

Persons who are biologically addicted to methamphetamine will start to experience withdrawal symptoms 4 to 8 hours after use. These symptoms are similar to that of cocaine withdrawals. These include:

- Severe depression
- Paranoia
- Irritability
- Lethargy
- Mental confusion
- Memory loss
- Suicide

SUMMARY

Horizontal Gaze Nystagmus	*No*
Vertical Gaze Nystagmus	*No*
Non-Convergence	*No*
Pupil Size	*Dilated*
Pupillary Reaction to Light	*Slow*
Pulse Rate	*Up*
Blood Pressure	*Up*
Body Temperature	*Up*
Muscle Tone	*Rigid*
Romberg Exam	*Fast*

PHENCYCLIDINE (PCP)

BACKGROUND

Encountering persons under the influence of PCP presents some very unique dangers to law enforcement personnel. These dangers include violent encounters with persons under the influence of the drug, and the dangers of contamination from the drug itself. Because of this, PCP will be examined in great detail.

Chemically, PCP is 1-(1-Phencyclohexyl) Piperidine Hydrochloride, and is the prototype of the various phencyclidines. There are some 34 analogs (drugs chemically similar) of PCP and an estimated 120 variations of those analogs which could be chemically produced. Therefore, these analogs, when introduced into the bloodstream, will produce basically the same effects.

Phencyclidine is a very powerful synthetic hallucinogen which was medically developed in the mid-1950's as an analgesic and anesthetic agent for primate research. In 1963, Parke-Davis marketed PCP under the brand name of Sernyl and it was used as a general anesthetic for human surgery. However, during the period of 1963 to 1965, medical personnel observed numerous unpredictable side effects which caused considerable concern. Many patients experienced mind-altering episodes which resulted in bizarre reactions and post-operative behavioral toxicity resulting in injuries to patients and hospital personnel. These complications forced Parke-Davis to discontinue the drug for human use in 1965, however, they did continue to utilize it as a veterinary tranquilizer under the brand name of Sernylan.

Ketamine, an analog of PCP, has recently emerged as a popular drug of abuse in the party and nightclub scene. Often referred to as "Special K," this drug has legitimate medical uses as an anesthetic in pediatric surgery and for use with burn victims.

RECOGNITION

- *Powder* - A crystalline substance which is usually white, off-white, or yellow in color, and emits an odor similar to that of ether. PCP powder is often referred to as "Crystal" or "Dust."

- *Liquid* - A straw-colored or light yellow liquid which is contained in various sized glass containers, which also emits a strong ether like odor. Liquid PCP is often referred to as "Juice."

- *Joint* - A hand-rolled cigarette or "pinroll" joint containing a leafy substance such as mint leaves, parsley, or marijuana. The PCP powder or liquid is either sprinkled or sprayed onto the smoking material. These are usually referred to as "PCP joints" or "Angel Dust joints."

- *Dipped Cigarette* - Commercially produced cigarettes such as Sherman, More, and Kool brands are dipped into liquid PCP, then dried and smoked. These are referred to as "Sherms" or "Super Kools."

- *Tablets* - Although these are very rare today, PCP tablets have been produced in home laboratories and have appeared on the street in almost every size and color including white, yellow, pink, and brown. Tablets have been referred to as "Peace Pills" and "Gorilla Biscuits."

PCP

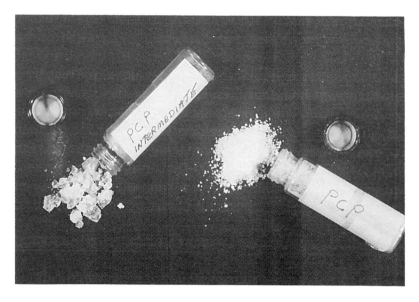

PCP (Intermediate and final stages)

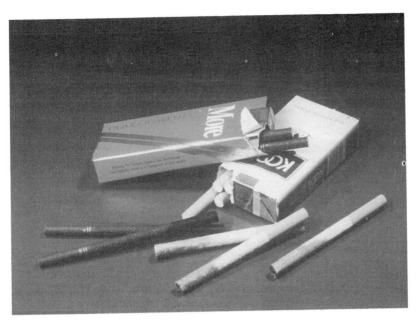

Cigarettes dipped in Liquid PCP

METHODS OF INGESTION

In the late 1960's, PCP surfaced on the streets of San Francisco in pill form and was known as the "Peace Pill." Shortly thereafter, the drug became available in powder and liquid form and was used mostly in smoking material when mixed with leafy material or when commercially produced cigarettes were dipped in liquid PCP. Although smoking is the most common method of using PCP, it can be swallowed, snorted, or injected. Today, it is found mostly in powder and liquid forms to be used with smoking material.

STREET SLANG

- A.D.
- Angel Dust
- Cannabinol
- Crystal
- Dust
- Elephant Tranquilizer
- Gorilla Biscuits
- Hog
- Juice
- Killerweed
- K.J.
- Lovely
- Mint Dew
- Peace Pills
- Rocket Fuel
- Shermans
- Sherms
- Special K
- Super Kools
- THC (Tetrahydrocannabinol)
- Trank
- Whack

Note: PCP users are normally referred to as "Dusters" or "Sherm Heads."

SYMPTOMATOLOGY (OVERVIEW)

Although Phencyclidine is a hallucinogenic drug, it can act as a stimulant in low doses, and as a depressant in higher doses. PCP causes a chemical imbalance in the brain and often produces psychotic or schizophrenic behavior. Schizophrenia or psychotic disorder is characterized by loss of contact with reality and the environment and by disintegration of personality, feeling, thought, and conduct. There are usually the presence of contradictory sensual stimuli, which commonly result in confusion and antagonism. This is characteristically followed by depression, fear, paranoia, violent behavior, delusions, and auditory as well as visual hallucinations. This entire psychotic episode can last from two or more hours to several days or even weeks.

PCP moves from the bloodstream into the adipose or fat tissues of the body as well as the brain tissues where it is stored for an indefinite period of time. Stress and other unpredictable factors may cause the stored PCP to be released back into the bloodstream causing re-intoxication, which is properly known as a recurring psychotic episode. These episodes are sometimes referred to as "flashbacks," however; they are, for the most part, recurring states of intoxication. A very serious concern about the indefinite storage of PCP in the adipose tissues is that former users or persons who had been exposed to the drug may possess it in their tissues for life. There are documented cases of persons who have passed the drug on from one generation to the next. This is a major reason for law enforcement personnel to be extremely cautious in handling PCP and the various precursor chemicals.

The user's level of intoxication will vary with the strength of the drug, the amount taken, the level of tolerance, the user's state of mind, and the external stimuli at the time of use. PCP can affect the user in many ways, however, the following listed symptoms are those which will be present most of the time in various combinations.

EYES

- *Pupils* - PCP will not usually have any impact on the pupil size. However, according to Dr. Forest Tennant (1991), PCP may cause pupillary constriction in some individuals.

- *Nystagmus* - Horizontal gaze nystagmus and vertical gaze nystagmus are symptoms that are normally present in every user under the influence of PCP.

- *Non-Convergence* - This is also usually present.

STIMULANT EFFECTS

Smaller amounts of PCP can affect the user as a central nervous system stimulant and symptoms usually include, but are not limited to, any of the following:

- *Blood Pressure* - Elevated blood pressure almost always occurs with PCP intoxication.

- *Elevated Pulse Rate* - (over 90 beats per minute)

- *Increased Respiration* - (over 20 breaths per minute)

- *Increased Body Temperature* - (over 98.6 degrees)

DEPRESSANT EFFECTS

Moderate to large amounts of PCP will affect the user as a central nervous system depressant and may result in outward signs of sedation and stuporous behavior. The symptoms usually include, but are not limited to, any of the following:

- Intoxicated appearance
- Slow and deliberate speech
- Slow and deliberate movements
- Poor motor coordination
- Poor depth perception
- High-stepping
- Lethargic appearance
- Droopy eyelids
- Communication problems
- Speaking in non-sequiturs
- Difficulty following instruction

GAIT ATAXIA

This limited motor coordination may include staggering, stumbling, and other forms of impaired pedestrian functions.

MUSCLE RIGIDITY

Muscle rigidity is quite common with PCP users, as they often tend to stiffen their muscles when moving or when reacting to physical force or restraint. This is most noticeable when a user is walking with a stiff, unyielding gait.

BLANK STARE APPEARANCE

This is a zombie-like stare during which the user appears to be looking right through you with a blank, but piercing stare. This eerie appearance tends to portray the user in a macabre, ghostly manner. This unsettling stare is, for the most part, caused by the user's severely impaired sensory perception and inability to comprehend.

ANALGESIA OR ANESTHESIA

This quality renders the user impervious to pain. Larger amounts can result in loss of sensation and perception with or without loss of consciousness.

AMNESIA

This feature involves a significant memory loss and the user may have difficulty remembering what occurred during the period of intoxication.

HALLUCINATIONS AND VISUAL DISTORTIONS

It is common for the user to have visual and auditory hallucinations, which can be very frightening. These hallucinations may include out-of-body experiences when they may see their body or head in a separate location from where they are actually standing or sitting. Religious and death-related hallucinations are fairly common, as they may believe they are God or the Devil, or acting on their behalf. Also characteristic are visual distortions when the users may see their limbs inflated, their bodies distorted, or a total distortion of everything around them.

AGITATION

The user is easily agitated, especially when introduced to sensory stimulation such as visual, tactile, and auditory enhancement. Lights appear to be brighter and sounds are louder which can easily change a calm user into an agitated or violent one.

ACUTE PARANOIA

This symptom can be described as a psychosis characterized by delusions of persecution or grandeur, with or without hallucinations. They become excessively suspicious and distrustful of others.

POOR DEPTH PERCEPTION

Due to the impaired sensory perception, the users have difficulty gauging the 3-dimensional relationship of objects including the relationship of their own bodies to the ground and the surrounding environment. This often results in the user high stepping and sometimes getting down on hands and knees in order to feel the ground.

NUDITY

A classic symptom, and one easily recognizable, is that of nudity. The reasons vary from the clothing being too restrictive to the heat from the increased body temperature. In any case, a nude person in a public place, acting in a bizarre fashion is a dead give-away.

SEEKING OUT WATER

Due to the increased body temperature and the possibility of a burning sensation on the skin, users often seek out water. This may result in a drowning because of the impaired sensory perception, poor motor coordination, and the contradictory sensual stimuli. The County Coroner should automatically screen all drowning victims for PCP.

SMASHING GLASS

This symptom is the result of confusion, anger, acute paranoia, and a distorted observation of life-sized, mirrored images, which may appear to be threatening.

ANIMAL NOISES AND ANIMAL MIMICRY

Growling, barking, and whining are among the many animal noises emitted from PCP users. In addition, many users envision themselves as wild animals and mimic them accordingly.

DROOLING AND SLOBBERING

Drooling saliva from the mouth coupled with incoherent utterances add to the list of other unpleasant symptoms.

VOMITING

A combination of PCP, anxiety, excitement, and physical exertion seem to influence this symptom.

SOBBING

The confusion, fear, lack of control, and vividly terrifying imagination make it a frightening experience which may lead to sobbing.

NOSE BLEEDS

On occasion, the hypertension and the violent activity can cause nosebleeds.

SELF MUTILATION

Psychosis, hallucinations, and the analgesic protection from pain have caused users to mutilate themselves, not to mention the severing of one's penis. This often occurs when users have had previous mental illness.

SUICIDE

Most users who appear to commit suicide don't always do so intentionally. The vast majority of deaths are caused by "behavioral toxicity" which is a euphemism for acting in a foolishly dangerous manner resulting in death.

VIOLENT, BIZARRE BEHAVIOR

Due to the unpredictable, psychotic effects of PCP, violence seems to be the behavior du jour when the user experiences a bad trip. The confusion, paranoia, hallucinations, and visual distortions may tend to reduce the intoxicating episode to one of violence and bizarre activity.

SUPER-HUMAN STRENGTH

The explanation of super-human strength is one of the most talked about mysteries of PCP intoxication. First of all, super-human strength does occur among some users as the result of a series of PCP-related phenomena.

(1) If you have ever seen anyone hypnotized, you probably saw that person perform amazing feats. If the hypnotist instructs the subjects to act like chickens, they do so. In other words, it is a question of mind over matter. One of these authors has seen a subject who was hypnotized and stretched out in a supine position between two metal chairs

with shoulders on one chair and heels on another and with no support for the torso. He was told that he was a steel beam and could not bend. This author and two other men sat on the subject's torso with full weight, and he did not bend. He really believed that he was a steel beam.

PCP has a similar hypnotic effect on the mind in that the intoxicated person will perform amazing acts which, under normal circumstances, could not have been possible.

(2) The user may have an exaggerated fear of things like snakes, monsters or any other creatures or things. The PCP user may see you and others as those terrifying creatures who have come to destroy him. Mentally, it is really happening and the fear is raging. The adrenaline flows and the user will have to fight to the finish in order to survive.

(3) Since PCP is a strong analgesic, the user will feel no pain at all and will not be affected by common bullet wounds and assaults with deadly weapons. So in this situation, pain compliance will be absolutely ineffective.

(4) The final and most potent ingredient to this bizarre mystery is the presence of a muscle enzyme called Creatinine Phospo Kinase or CPK.

Under normal conditions, a sober person's blood may produce a reading of less than 220 units. When a person is under severe physical stress and is exhibiting the psychotic, schizophrenic violent behavior and is being physically restrained, the user's CPK level could reach several thousand units. This has resulted in strength that has snapped metal handcuffs and thick leather restraints. In the case of metal handcuffs, it required 550 pounds of pressure to break the cuffs. So, it is not a myth.

Super-human strength has become a serious issue, especially when one individual has the ability to over-power several, often larger, police officers.

Broken Handcuffs caused by PCP Suspect

ROMBERG EXAM

Persons under the influence of PCP will display a distorted Romberg. This is due to having major difficulty in determining time. The results could be rapid or delayed.

DURATION OF EFFECTS

The amount of time that PCP remains in the blood is unpredictable. Although it will usually be present in the blood within two to four hours, and remain for 48 hours or more, it is not always detectable. Since the drug hides in the adipose tissues, the only way to accurately determine if the subject has

PCP in his/her system is to draw several blood samples over a 24-hour period.

Gas chromatography/mass spectrometry is an excellent method of quantitatively measuring phencyclidine as well as utilizing some radioimmunoassays for its detection and identification.

An additional complication is the fact that the long list of analogs will not normally be identified as phencyclidine because each analog often requires its own specific screening in order to be detected. Therefore, if the user is under the influence of a PCP analog, the screening for phencyclidine will probably result in a negative finding.

URINALYSIS

PCP involves liver metabolism and renal excretion, thereby causing elimination of the drug through the urine. Although PCP is normally present in the urine within minutes of use, it may not be detected for four to six hours or even days later depending on the pH factor. Since the drug is chemically a weak base, the acidification process will hasten the appearance of PCP in the urine, therefore, numerous urine samples over an extended period is also recommended.

Due to the fact that PCP is lipid soluble, it is rapidly distributed into adipose tissues, which may have higher concentrations of the drug than in the blood or brain. Some researchers have discovered that the highest concentrations may be found in the gastric juices.

WITHDRAWAL

- Memory Loss
- Confusion
- Headaches
- Depression

- Paranoia
- Irritability
- Suicidal Tendencies
- Recurring Psychotic Episodes
- Post Drug Impairment Syndrome (PDIS)

CONTROLLING THE PCP USER

In controlling the PCP user, officer safety is paramount. There are also many factors which must be considered when confronting a PCP user including the personality of the user (calm or violent), the danger that the user presents to others, the physical setting and environment at the scene, the number of physically-capable officers present, the temperament of the bystanders (supportive or hostile toward police), the amount of training and experience of the officers, policies and procedures of the agency involved, and the tools at hand for a successful outcome.

Without presenting a detailed, procedural explanation of every possible tactic which could be utilized, the following list includes a wide range of options:

- Talking the user down
- Swarm technique (using several physically-capable officers and body weight)
- Upper body control holds
- Taser or stun gun
- Electronic dart gun
- Large restraining net
- Deadly force (Firearm)

Various types of tear gas (CN or CS) and pepper sprays are usually ineffective in immobilizing PCP users, but can be used as a diversionary tactic.

CHEMICALS AND CLANDESTINE LABORATORIES

A significant danger is always present when law enforcement personnel have contact with chemicals and clandestine laboratories. It can be hazardous to handle any of the chemicals or to breathe the fumes without the proper protective apparatus. Perhaps the most dangerous characteristic of most illicit laboratories is that of ether fumes which frequently fill the air in and around the structure. A tiny flame from a water heater or stove, a burning end of a cigarette, or even a spark from a light switch could ignite the volatile ether fumes, which will result in a damaging explosion. It is always advisable to have a Hazardous Material (Haz-Mat) team at the location in addition to the fire department. The only other personnel who should be at the scene are trained investigators and criminalists who may be needed for conducting the investigation and securing the evidence.

The following is a list of common precursor chemicals used in the manufacturing of phencyclidine:

- *Piperidine* - This is a straw colored liquid which emits an odor similar to ammonia.

- *Cyclohexanone* - This is a clear liquid which emits an odor similar to glue.

- *Ethyl Ether or Petroleum Ether* - This is a clear liquid with a distinct odor, which is extremely flammable.

- *Sodium Cyanide or Potassium Cyanide* - White crystalline material. When mixed with hydrochloric acid it produces a deadly, poisonous gas.

- *Hydrochloric Acid* - This is a clear liquid. When mixed with sodium cyanide or potassium cyanide, it produces a deadly, poisonous gas.

- *Sodium Bisulfite* – This is a white crystalline material.

- *Bromobenzine* – This is a clear liquid.

- *Magnesium Turnings or Shavings* – These are gray metal chips.

- *Iodine Crystals* – These are dark purple shiny crystals.

- *Sodium Carbonate* – This is a white powder.

- *Sodium Hydrozine (Lye)* –This is a white shiny crystalline material.

Clandestine Laboratory

Clandestine Laboratory

SUMMARY

Horizontal Gaze Nystagmus	*Yes*
Vertical Gaze Nystagmus	*Yes*
Non-Convergence	*Yes*
Pupil Size	*Normal*
Pupillary Reaction to Light	*Normal*
Pulse Rate	*Up*
Blood Pressure	*Up*
Body Temperature	*Up*
Muscle Tone	*Rigid*
Romberg Exam	*Fast or Distorted*

LSD (LYSERGIC ACID DIETHYLAMIDE)

BACKGROUND

LSD is a powerful hallucinogen that was first produced in 1938. It is a semisynthetic derivative of the ergot alkaloids obtained from *Claviceps Purpurea*, the fungus that grows on various types of grains, especially rye and wheat (Radcliffe et al 1994). It was widely used as a psychotherapeutic agent, made infamous in 1962, by Dr. Timothy Leary doing LSD experimentation at Harvard University. The drug was not controlled until 1965. Currently there is no legitimate medical use for LSD.

RECOGNITION

In the 1960's, LSD was marketed in a pill form. These pills were orange in color and called *Orange Sunshine*.

In recent years LSD is almost exclusively sold in blotter form. Liquid LSD is sprayed or soaked on to paper, (about 1/4 inch square) usually bearing a logo or some type of a cartoon character. LSD can also be found in a clear liquid, or even a powdered form.

METHODS OF INGESTION

LSD is usually taken orally, the "tab" or "hit" is placed under the tongue and allowed to absorb. Liquid LSD is also taken orally or sublingual. LSD can also be absorbed through the skin. Some users even apply it directly to the eyeball.

LSD Tabs

STREET SLANG

- Acid
- Windowpane
- Blotter
- Micro-dot
- Tab
- Purple haze
- LSD

METHODS OF PACKAGING

- Cellophane
- Bindles
- Tin foil
- Glass vials
- Eyedropper bottles

SYMPTOMATOLOGY (OVERVIEW)

Like PCP, LSD causes a chemical imbalance in the brain. The effects of LSD are extremely unpredictable. When orally ingested, the effects of the drug will be produced within 30 to 45 minutes.

EYES

- *Pupils* - LSD will cause the pupils to dilate over 6.5 mm. Oftentimes the pupils will get so large that they are referred to as "saucer eyes."

- *Reaction to Light* - LSD may cause the pupil to be slow in reacting to the absence or presence of light.

- *Hippus* - may be present

- *Rebound Dilation* - may be present

- *Other Conditions* - LSD will not usually cause nystagmus, or non-convergence.

STIMULANT EFFECTS

- *Increased Heart Rate* - over 90 beats per minute
- *Elevated Blood Pressure* - over 140/90
- *High Body Temperature* - over 98.6 degrees
- *Rapid Respiration* - over 20 breaths per minute

ROMBERG EXAM

Persons under the influence of LSD will display a distorted Romberg; it could be rapid or delayed.

HALLUCINATIONS

Hallucinations associated with LSD intoxication tend to be sensory in nature, with vision being the most affected. This may be due to the stimulation of an organ in the brain called the *Reticular Formation*, which plays an important role in the formulation of perception.

Users report seeing things in great detail, with color and texture being extremely vivid. Users also claim that they see "after images." For instance if a person walks out of a room, the image of the person may still be present.

LSD intoxication can also cause an overlapping of the senses. People say that they hear colors and see sounds while under the influence of LSD. This crossing over of the senses is referred to as *synesthesia*.

LSD will usually enhance the mood or emotional condition that the person is experiencing prior to taking the drug. However other prominent effects seen with LSD are feelings of depersonalization, a loss of body image, and loss of a sense of reality (Radcliffe et al 1994). Oftentimes extreme fear or panic is associated with bad LSD "trips."

Flashbacks have been reported for up to two years after use. There are three different types of flashbacks.

- *Emotional* - These are usually associated with feelings of fear and panic.
- *Somatic* - The user will experience altered body sensations.
- *Perceptual* - The user will experience sensory distortions.

OTHER OBJECTIVE SYMPTOMS

- Goose flesh (Piloerection)
- Decreased muscular coordination
- Tremors of the fingers and hands
- Muscular contractions (caused by stimulation of the muscles)

77

- Swings in mood and emotion
- Nausea
- Dizziness
- Feelings of depersonalization
- Distorted perceptions
- Anxiety
- Organic defects (brain damage)
- Death

DURATION OF EFFECTS

LSD stays active in the body 7 to 12 hours after use. However, drug induced psychotic episodes associated with "bad trips" may last for several years.

WITHDRAWAL

- Anxiety
- Restlessness
- Chills
- Nausea
- Depression

These symptoms will usually last for up to 24 hours. LSD is not biologically addicting in the same way as heroin or cocaine, yet users report severe depression within a few days after the last use.

SUMMARY

Horizontal Gaze Nystagmus	*No*
Vertical Gaze Nystagmus	*No*
Non-Convergence	*No*
Pupil Size	*Dilated*
Pupillary Reaction to Light	*Slow*

Pulse Rate	*Up*
Blood Pressure	*Up*
Body Temperature	*Up*
Muscle Tone	*Rigid*
Romberg Exam	*Fast or Distorted*

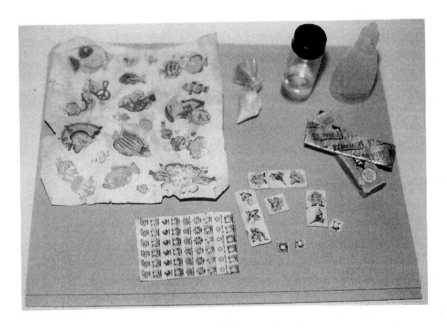

LSD

PSILOCYBIN

BACKGROUND

There are about twenty different species of mushrooms that contain psilocybin or psilocin, which is a strong mind-altering or hallucinogenic drug. The Aztecs and other Indian civilizations have used psilocybin ceremonially, dating as far back as 1500 B.C.

These mushrooms grow naturally, but are also commercially cultivated for street sales. Psilocybin spores can be purchased along with cultivation kits. With a few glass jars, one can produce a considerable amount of mushrooms.

RECOGNITION

Psilocybin mushrooms are similar in appearance to the common mushroom. The top or cap of the mushroom varies in color from a light tan or gold, to white. The outer edge of the cap is a darker gold color. The caps of the mushrooms vary from ½" to 2" in diameter, with some as large as 5". When the mushrooms are dried, they shrivel and appear dark brown in color.

METHODS OF INGESTION

Mushrooms can be eaten, or the mushroom can be ground up and swallowed in capsule form. Mushrooms can also be broken up and rolled in marijuana cigarettes or mixed in with other smoking material.

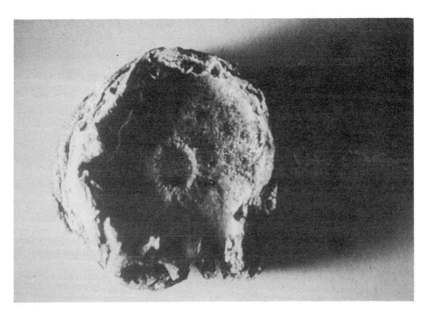

Psilocybin Mushroom

Psilocybin Mushrooms

STREET SLANG

- Magic mushrooms
- Shrooms
- Caps
- Psilocybin
- Psilocin

METHODS OF PACKAGING

- Cellophane baggies
- Clear capsules

SYMPTOMATOLOGY (OVERVIEW)

Psilocybin or Psilocin is a strong mind-altering or halluci-nogenic drug. The effects will peak in about 30 minutes, and are very similar to that of LSD. The user will experience a stimulation of the central nervous system, vivid sensory perception and visual imagery.

EYES

- *Pupil Dilation* - Psilocybin will cause the pupils to dilate over 6.5 mm.

- *Reaction to Light* - Psilocybin may cause the pupil to be slow in reacting to the absence or presence of light.

- *Hippus* - may be present

- *Rebound Dilation* - may be present

- *Other Conditions* - Psilocybin will not cause nystagmus or non-convergence.

STIMULANT EFFECTS

- *Increased Heart Rate* - over 90 beats per minute
- *Elevated Blood Pressure* - over 140/90
- *High Body Temperature* - over 98.6 degrees
- *Rapid Respiration* - over 20 breaths per minute

ROMBERG EXAM

A person under the influence of psilocybin may display a distorted Romberg; it could be rapid or delayed.

HALLUCINATIONS

Like LSD, hallucinations while under the influence of psilocybin tend to be sensory in nature. Some users report an enhanced feeling of love and affection. Other users report experiencing feeling of anxiety and panic.

OTHER OBJECTIVE SYMPTOMS

- Decreased muscular coordination
- Swings in mood and emotion
- Nausea
- Dizziness
- Feelings of depersonalization
- Distorted perceptions
- Organic defects (brain damage)
- Euphoria
- Severe confusion
- Suicide
- Death

DURATION OF EFFECTS

Symptoms of influence will last 2 to 24 hours after use, depending on the dose taken. Like other hallucinogens, psychological disorders could be long lasting or even permanent.

SUMMARY

Horizontal Gaze Nystagmus	No
Vertical Gaze Nystagmus	No
Non-Convergence	No
Pupil Size	Dilated
Pupillary Reaction to Light	Slow
Pulse Rate	Up
Blood Pressure	Up
Body Temperature	Up
Muscle Tone	Rigid
Romberg Exam	Fast or Distorted

PEYOTE/MESCALINE

BACKGROUND

Mescaline is a hallucinogenic alkaloid of the Peyote Cactus. The Aztecs, who named the Peyote Cactus, were among the first people to utilize Mescaline as a hallucinogenic drug. American, Mexican, and Central American Indians have used it in religious ceremonies since pre-Christian times.

As of 1954, one half of all Native American Indians still used Peyote. In 1964, the California Supreme Court ruled that Native American Indians could use Peyote for religious purposes, and its use is protected under the First Amendment to the U.S. Constitution; freedom of religion. However, its use is restricted to specific ceremonies on designated Indian land. In 1990 the U.S. Supreme Court ruled (U.S. Supreme Court, No. 88-1214, 4/17/97, 47 CrLr 2001) that the individual states could apply its own standards to the enforcement of Peyote to those persons using the drug for religious purposes.

RECOGNITION

Peyote is spineless cactus with a crown or button usually two or three inches in diameter, with a long carrot-like root. The button is cut off, allowed to dry, and resembles a hard brown disk or button.

METHODS OF INGESTION

Peyote buttons are chewed, or sometimes it is brewed into a tea. Some users will grind up the buttons, put it in gelatin capsules, and swallow them.

STREET SLANG

- Mescaline
- Buttons
- Cactus

METHODS OF PACKAGING

- Cellophane baggies
- Tin foil

SYMPTOMATOLOGY (OVERVIEW)

Mescaline is a mind-altering drug very similar to that of LSD or Psilocybin. After ingesting the peyote, the user will often experience nausea and vomiting. This is usually followed by a stimulation of the central nervous system, and intense visual hallucinations.

EYES

- *Pupil Dilation* - over 6.5 mm.

- *Reaction to Light* - Peyote may cause the pupil to be slow in reacting to the absence or presence of light.

- *Hippus* - may be present

- *Rebound Dilation* - may be present

- *Other Conditions* - Peyote will not cause nystagmus or non-convergence.

STIMULANT EFFECTS

- *Increased Heart Rate* - over 90 beats per minute
- *Elevated Blood Pressure* - over 140/90
- *High Body Temperature* - over 98.6 degrees
- *Rapid Respiration* - over 20 breaths per minute

ROMBERG EXAM

A person under the influence of peyote may display a distorted Romberg; it could be rapid or delayed.

HALLUCINATIONS

Peyote/Mescaline can cause hallucinations very similar to that of LSD and Psilocybin. Hallucinations caused by Peyote are said to be spiritual and introspective in nature.

OTHER OBJECTIVE SYMPTOMS

- Decreased muscular coordination
- Mood swings
- Nausea
- Dizziness
- Feelings of depersonalization
- Distorted perceptions
- Organic defects (brain damage)
- Euphoria
- Suicide
- Death

DURATION OF EFFECTS

The effects of Peyote will last for 10 to 12 hours.

SUMMARY

Horizontal Gaze Nystagmus	*No*
Vertical Gaze Nystagmus	*No*
Non-Convergence	*No*
Pupil Size	*Dilated*
Pupillary Reaction to Light	*Slow*
Pulse Rate	*Up*

Blood Pressure	*Up*
Body Temperature	*Up*
Muscle Tone	*Rigid*
Romberg Exam	*Fast or Distorted*

Peyote

Marijuana-Laced Brownies and Cookies

Marijuana

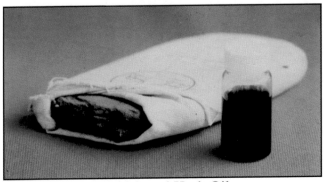

Hashish and Hash Oil

Packaged Heroin

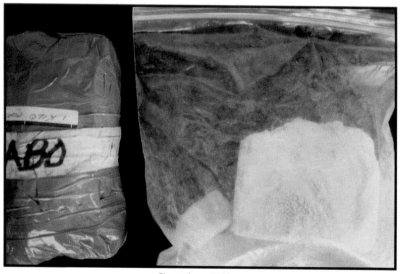

Cocaine Kilos

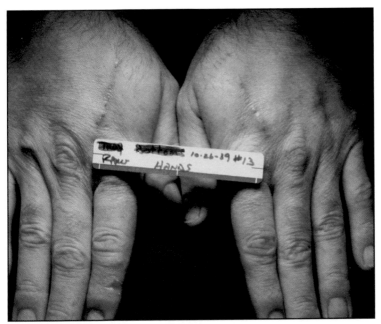

Tracks

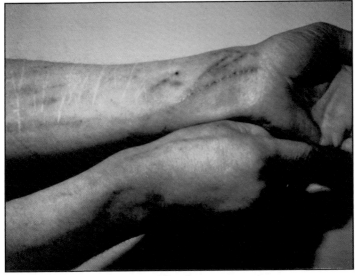

Tracks

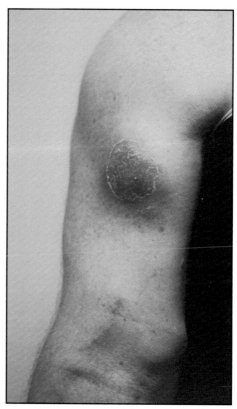

Abscessed areas caused by puncture wounds

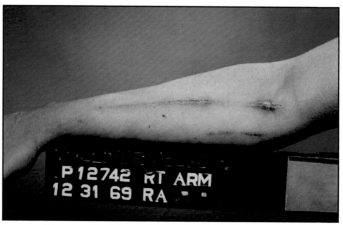

Tracks from numerous puncture wounds

LSD Tabs

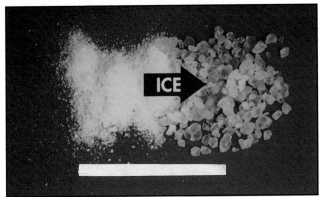

Methamphetamine (Ice-Freebase form)

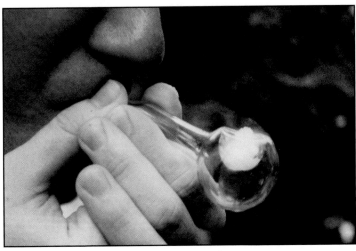

Methamphetamine

Cocaine (Cut and Pure)

Cocaine kilos and Marijuana kilos
inside suitcase

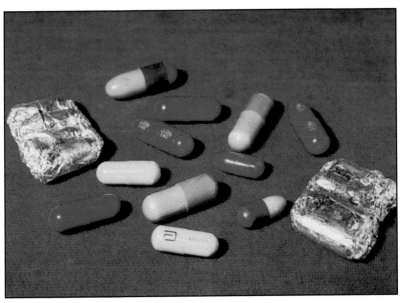

Barbiturates

Dextroamphetamine (Dexedrine and Dexamyl)

Opium Poppy

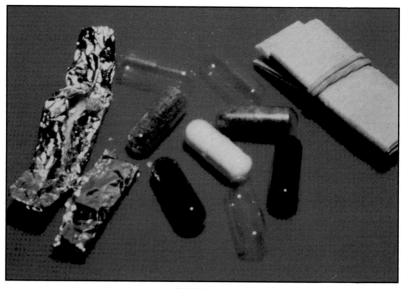

MDMA

MDMA (3,4-METHYLENDIOXY-METHAMPHETAMINE)

BACKGROUND

MDMA is a synthetic analog of the drug MDA, which was widely researched and used in the late 1960's and early 1970's as an adjunct to psychotherapy. MDA was also widely abused, often called the *Mellow Drug of America*.

MDMA combines the effects of methamphetamine and psilocybin, and it is often called the "love drug." It is said to act as an aphrodisiac, causing warm and affectionate feelings between friends. There is no medical use for MDMA (or MDA), and its source is from clandestine laboratories.

RECOGNITION

MDMA may appear in many forms. This includes:

- Clear liquid
- White powder
- Brown powder
- Blotter or tabs (similar to LSD)
- Pills or tablets in any shape or color
- Gelatin capsules

METHODS OF INGESTION

- Pill form - The pills or capsules are swallowed. These pills are often times colored and made to look like candy.

- Liquid form - In liquid form, the MDMA can be taken orally. Often times the dose is dispensed with a spray bottle into the mouth of the user. MDMA can also be mixed with an alcoholic beverage and drunk.

- Blotter or tab form – When in this form, it is taken orally like LSD.

- Powder form – When in powder form, MDMA can be snorted, smoked, injected, or consumed orally.

STREET SLANG

- MDMA
- Ecstasy
- X
- Rave
- XTC
- Adam
- Love drug

METHODS OF PACKAGING

Because of its many forms, MDMA can be packaged in many ways.

- Cellophane baggies
- Paper bindles
- Glass vials
- Gelatin capsules
- Concealed in bags of candy
- Inserted inside of soft candy

SYMPTOMATOLOGY (OVERVIEW)

MDMA is a psychedelic amphetamine, which causes symptoms consistent with high doses of amphetamine influence. It also causes symptoms consistent with mushroom/psilocybin intoxication.

Most likely persons under the influence of MDMA will be hyperactive, displaying symptoms of methamphetamine intoxication, and be highly euphoric or even affectionate. They also grind their teeth which is known as bruxism. In order to prevent total tooth destruction, users will often suck on a baby pacifier or some type of candied sucker. Some users may be seen wearing a pacifier on a necklace or a pacifier-type ring. Other users may carry mentholated rubs or inhalers for they report that the fumes enhance the "high." The additive effect of these fumes has not been established.

EYES

- *Pupil Dilation* - over 6.5 mm

- *Reaction to Light* - MDMA may cause the pupil to be slow in reacting to the absence or presence of light

- *Hippus* - may be present

- *Rebound Dilation* - may be present

- *Other Conditions* - MDMA will not cause nystagmus, or non-convergence

STIMULANT EFFECTS

- *Increased Heart Rate* - over 90 beats per minute
- *Elevated Blood Pressure* - over 140/90
- *High Body Temperature* - over 98.6 degrees
- *Rapid Respiration* - over 20 breaths per minute

ROMBERG EXAM

A person under the influence of MDMA will usually display a rapid Romberg.

HALLUCINATIONS

Few users of MDMA report experiencing the intense visual or auditory hallucinations which are often experienced with other types of hallucinogens. MDMA is said to produce a deep sense of physical well-being, increased sensations of touch, and, in some, an increased desire to be with other people (Radcliffe et al, 1994).

OTHER OBJECTIVE SYMPTOMS

- Decreased muscular coordination
- Mood swings
- Hyperactivity
- Dizziness
- Disorientation
- Distorted perceptions
- Organic defects (brain damage)
- Euphoria
- Suicide
- Death

SUMMARY

Horizontal Gaze Nystagmus	*No*
Vertical Gaze Nystagmus	*No*
Non-Convergence	*No*
Pupil Size	*Dilated*
Pupillary Reaction to Light	*Slow*
Pulse Rate	*Up*
Blood Pressure	*Up*
Body Temperature	*Up*
Muscle Tone	*Rigid*
Romberg Exam	*Fast or Distorted*

BUFOTENINE

BACKGROUND

Bufotenine is a natural organic compound produced in the glands of over 62 species of Bufo or Cane toads. This is a protective substance that is excreted by the toad to protect itself from predators. The Colorado River Toad is the most common species used for drug ingestion.

Colorado River Toad

RECOGNITION

Bufotenine, when excreted from the toad, is a white milky substance.

METHODS OF INGESTION

The user will lick the excretions off of the toad. Some users report that this method of consumption makes them ill. Another user reported milking the glands of the toad and smoking it in a similar fashion as crack cocaine.

STREET SLANG

- Bufo
- Toad Butts

SYMPTOMATOLOGY

Bufotenine is a very powerful hallucinogen. The effects of bufotenine are similar to that of LSD. As one user described it, ... *"If LSD was milk, bufotenine would be like Whiskey,"* (Campy, 1994).

SUMMARY

Horizontal Gaze Nystagmus	*No*
Vertical Gaze Nystagmus	*No*
Non-Convergence	*No*
Pupil Size	*Dilated*
Pupillary Reaction to Light	*Slow*
Pulse Rate	*Up*
Blood Pressure	*Up*
Body Temperature	*Up*
Muscle Tone	*Rigid*
Romberg Exam	*Fast or Distorted*

MARIJUANA

BACKGROUND

Marijuana is the common name for Cannabis Sativa L. or the Indian Hemp plant. Marijuana grows well in most tropical and temperate climates. Some of the best marijuana in the world is grown in Northern California.

The chemical in marijuana, which produces the greatest mood-altering effects, is Delta-9-Tetrahydrocannabinol (THC). Marijuana use was prohibited in the United States after 1937. There continues to be medical research with the use of marijuana in the treatment of vomiting and nausea sometimes caused by chemotherapy, for the treatment of glaucoma, pain relief, anorexia, and asthma.

Marijuana Plant

95

Marijuana Bud

__RECOGNITION__

- *Plant material* - The leaves or buds of the plant are harvested, dried, and range in color from a greenish-brown to a dark brown. The bud of the plant contains the highest percentage of THC.

- *Hash* or *Hashish* - This is a concentrated form of marijuana and appears in a solid form, usually brown in color.

- *Hash oil* - This is yet a higher concentrated form of marijuana, and is similar in appearance to motor oil. Hash oil is sometimes referred to as honey oil.

- *Marinol* (also known as Dronabinol), is a synthetically produced form of THC. It is used medically to treat persons who suffer nausea as a result of chemotherapy. Marinol comes in a pill or capsule form.

METHODS OF INGESTION

- *Smoked* - Marijuana is usually smoked from hand rolled cigarettes or out of pipes. Hash and hash oil is also smoked from pipes.

- *Orally* - Marijuana, hash, or hash oil can be put in gelatin capsules and swallowed, or mixed with food and eaten.

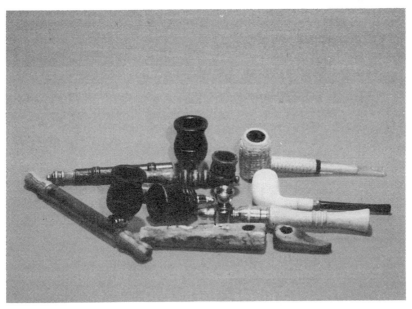

Hash Pipes

STREET SLANG

- Pot
- Weed
- Ganga
- Reefer
- Doobie
- Cronic
- Mota

- Herb
- Ses
- Grass
- MJ
- Smoke
- 420
- Joint

METHODS OF PACKAGING

- Rolled into cigarettes or joints
- Baggies
- Pound or kilo quantities can be compressed into bricks

SYMPTOMATOLOGY (OVERVIEW)

THC is a very powerful mind-altering drug, causing psycho-motor impairments for several days. Marijuana will cause changes in the neurotransmitters endorphin and norepineph-rine, along with other related hormones.

Marijuana is a very dangerous drug for it can have the effect of a hallucinogen, a stimulant, and a depressant. Marijuana use can cause biological addiction, and some users must smoke it every 2 to 4 hours.

EYES

- *Dilated Pupils* - Marijuana will usually dilate the pupils over 6.5 mm.

- *Reaction to Light* - Pupillary reaction to light, while under the influence of cannabis, will usually be normal.

- *Rebound Dilation* - may be present.

- *Hippus* - may be present.

- *Non-Convergence* - is almost always present within the first two hours after use.

- *Reddened Sclera* - Marijuana will cause very noticeable reddening of the eyes, as well as the tissue around the eyes.

STIMULANT EFFECTS

- *Rapid Pulse* - over 90 beats per minute
- *Elevated Blood Pressure* - over 140/90
- *Body Temperature* - will usually be normal
- *Rapid Respiration* - over 20 breaths per minute

ROMBERG EXAM

Persons under the influence cannabis will display a distorted Romberg; it could be rapid or delayed.

EUPHORIA

Within the first two hours of use, marijuana may cause an euphoric feeling or "high," along with a sense of relaxation or sedation.

MOTOR IMPAIRMENTS

Marijuana use severely impairs motor skills, and distorts one's ability to judge time, distance, and space. This condition may last for several days.

SHORT TERM MEMORY

Marijuana impairs the ability to recall information and process things from short-term into long-term memory. People under the influence of marijuana have a very difficult time with divided attention tasks, or doing multiple things at one time.

HALLUCINATIONS

Marijuana in very high doses has been reported to cause sensory hallucinations, and distorting perceptions of time, distance, and space.

SIGNS OF INGESTION

Marijuana has a very strong odor, which can often be detected on the person's breath and person. Because marijuana is a vegetable material, oftentimes a person will have a green tongue.

OTHER OBJECTIVE SYMPTOMS

- Memory loss
- Learning impairments
- Loss of energy
- Loss of motivation
- Decreased visual perception
- Sinusitis
- Bronchitis
- Impairment of the immune system
- Hypertension
- Decreased male masculinity (lowered testosterone levels)
- Infertility in males
- Gynecomastia (larger breasts in males due to decrease in testosterone level)
- Irregular menstrual cycles
- Increased level of testosterone in females causing decreased femininity

- Embryo toxicity (increased infant mortality rates)
- Reduced attention span
- Anxiety attacks

DURATION OF EFFECTS

Marijuana remains in the bloodstream for up to 5 days, much longer than heroin, cocaine or methamphetamine.

THC stays active in the body for approximately 2 to 3 hours. After this period of time, *THC* is metabolized into *Hydroxy THC*, which still causes the user to feel the effects for approximately six hours. The body continues to metabolize the marijuana into a third compound known as *Carboxy THC.* This final metabolite will stay active in the body for up to five days, still causing psychomotor impairments.

THC is fat soluble, and can be detected in the urine for up to 45 days after use.

WITHDRAWAL

If a person is biologically addicted to marijuana, withdrawal symptoms will start five days or less after the last use and will usually last for two weeks. Withdrawal symptoms will include:

- Anxiety
- Depression
- Paranoia
- Panic
- Sleeplessness
- Sweating
- Loss of appetite
- Nausea

SUMMARY

Horizontal Gaze Nystagmus	*No*
Vertical Gaze Nystagmus	*No*
Non-Convergence	*Yes*
Pupil Size	*Dilated*
Pupillary Reaction to Light	*Normal*
Pulse Rate	*Up*
Blood Pressure	*Up*
Body Temperature	*Normal*
Muscle Tone	*Normal*
Romberg Exam	*Distorted*

Marijuana (Thai sticks)

DEPRESSANTS (BARBITURATES/ SEDATIVES/TRANQUILIZERS)

BACKGROUND

Depressants have been used medically since 1903. With over 2,500 different types on the market, and with over 90,000,000 prescriptions written annually, more people are addicted to this category of drugs than all others combined.

Depressants suppress the functions of the central nervous system. This category of drugs actually contains several sub-categories. These include:

- *Barbiturates* – These are derivatives of barbituric acid and includes such compounds as Secobarbital (Seconal), Pentobarbital (Nembutal), Amosecobarbital (Tuinal), Amobarbital (Amytal), and Phenobarbital (Luminal).

- *Non-Barbiturates* – These are synthetic compounds, having similar effects as barbiturates. These include drugs like Chloral Hydrate, Doriden, Soma, Methaqualone and GHB.

- *Anti-Anxiety Tranquilizers* – These are perhaps the most widely abused drugs of this category and include Valium, Xanax, Klonopin, Rohypnol, and Ativan.

- *Anti-Depressants* – These are also known as mood elevators and include Prozac, Nardil and Elavil.

- *Anti-Psychotic Tranquilizers* – These are also referred to as major tranquilizers, and are often prescribed to persons with severe psychological or emotional disorders. These drugs include Lithium, Haldol, and Thyroxin.

- *Combinations* – These are mixtures of the above compounds, and include medications such as Travail and Libra.

MEDICAL USES

- Induce sleep
- Calm or tranquilize
- Prevent seizures
- Pain killers
- Mood elevators
- Relieve anxiety

RECOGNITION

Since most of the drugs in the *depressant* category are prescription medications, the *Physician's Desk Reference*, or other similar publications, are helpful in identifying the substance.

Many of these medications can also be found in generic form, and your local pharmacist can be of great assistance in identifying the drug.

METHODS OF INGESTION

- *Orally* – Since these drugs are usually in pill or capsule form, they are most commonly swallowed.

- *Injected* – The pills or capsules can be dissolved in water and injected.

STREET SLANG

- Reds (Secobarbital - Seconal)
- Yellow jackets (Pentobarbital - Nembutal)
- Rainbows (Amosecobarbital - Tuinal)
- Blues (Amobarbital - Amytal)
- Pink ladies (Phenobarbital - Luminal)

- Doors (Doriden)
- Ludes (Methaqualone)
- Downers (any depressant drug)
- Roofies/Date rape drug (Flunitrazepam - Rohypnol)

SYMPTOMATOLOGY (OVERVIEW)

A person intoxicated on depressants may appear to be drunk, or under the influence of an opiate. In fact, alcohol is considered a model depressant, but will be covered separately in the next chapter.

EYES

- *Pupils* - The pupils of a person under the influence of depressants will usually not be affected. The exception to this is with Soma, Quaaludes, Prozac, and MAO Inhibitors, which may dilate the pupils.

- *Reaction to Light* - The pupils will be sluggish in response to the absence or presence of light.

- *Nystagmus* - Depressants will usually cause both horizontal and vertical nystagmus.

- *Non-Convergence* - Depressants may also cause non-convergence.

- *Reddened Sclera* - Depressants may cause the eyes to appear bloodshot and watery.

- *Other Conditions* - Rebound dilation and hippus will not be present.

DEPRESSION OF CENTRAL NERVOUS SYSTEM

- *Slow Pulse Rate* - under 60 beats per minute (Quaaludes, Prozac, and MAO Inhibitors may elevate the pulse)

- *Lowered Blood Pressure* - under 120/70

- *Decreased Respiratory Rate* - under 20 breaths per minute

- *Body Temperature* - will usually be normal

ROMBERG EXAM

A person under the influence of a depressant will display a delayed Romberg.

OTHER SYMPTOMS

- Poor coordination
- Impaired judgment
- Euphoria
- Depression
- Gait ataxia
- Slurred speech
- Drowsiness
- Droopy eyelids
- Double vision

- Slowed reflexes
- Lethargy
- Mood swings
- Depression
- Confusion
- Brain damage
- Coma
- Death

SIGNS OF INGESTION

If these drugs are injected, the puncture wounds tend to swell and ulcerate.

DURATION OF EFFECTS

The onset and duration of depressants varies greatly, depending on the type of drug taken. The effects may last for only a few hours, or in the case of anti-seizure medications (Barbital), they can last for 8 to 14 hours.

WITHDRAWALS

People addicted to depressants may suffer severe withdrawal symptoms which could last for two weeks. These could include:

- Convulsions
- Deliriums
- Nightmares
- Coma
- Death

SUMMARY

Horizontal Gaze Nystagmus	*Yes*
Vertical Gaze Nystagmus	*Yes*
Non-Convergence	*Yes*
Pupil Size	*Normal (1)*
Pupillary Reaction to Light	*Slow*
Pulse Rate	*Down (2)*
Blood Pressure	*Down*
Body Temperature	*Normal*
Muscle Tone	*Flaccid*
Romberg Exam	*Delayed*

(1) *Soma, Quaaludes, and MAO Inhibitors may dilate the pupils.*
(2) *Soma, Quaaludes, and MAO Inhibitors may increase the pulse.*

ALCOHOL

BACKGROUND

Alcohol is abused by an estimated 40 to 50 million Americans. There are three types of alcohol:

- *Ethyl Alcohol (Ethanol)* - This is the ingestible form that causes intoxication.

- *Methyl Alcohol (Methanol)* - This is commonly referred to as wood alcohol.

- *Isopropyl Alcohol (Isopropanol)* - This is commonly known as rubbing alcohol.

For the purpose of determining intoxication, we are only concerned with the effects of ethyl alcohol (ethanol).

METHODS OF INGESTION

- *Orally* - Alcohol is obviously consumed orally. About 20% of the alcohol is absorbed directly by the walls of the stomach. The remaining 80% will be absorbed by the small intestine. From the stomach and intestine, the alcohol is absorbed directly into the blood.

- *Inhalation* - Prolonged breathing of concentrated fumes can also cause intoxication.

- *Injection* - Alcohol can also be injected, but this method is extremely rare.

SYMPTOMATOLOGY (OVERVIEW)

Alcohol is considered a model Central Nervous System Depressant, however in low doses it causes stimulation and euphoric effects. In higher doses it can cause sedation, depression, and even death.

EYES

- *Pupils* – Alcohol will not usually dilate the pupils over 6.5 mm, however persons under the influence of alcohol tend to have larger pupils.

- *Reaction to Light* – Alcohol will cause the pupils to react slowly to the absence and presence of light.

- *Nystagmus* – Alcohol will cause horizontal nystagmus. A Blood Alcohol Content of 0.05% (about two beers) will cause an onset of horizontal nystagmus at approximately 45 degrees.

- Vertical nystagmus will also be present in high doses for the individual user.

- *Non-Convergence* – This may also be present, particularly in higher doses.

- *Reddened Sclera* – Alcohol intoxication will usually cause the eyes to be bloodshot and watery.

- *Other Conditions* – Alcohol will not usually cause rebound dilation or hippus.

STIMULATION/DEPRESSION OF THE CENTRAL NERVOUS SYSTEM

- *Rapid Pulse* - Alcohol will elevate the pulse over 90 beats per minute.

- *Blood Pressure* - Alcohol, being a depressant, will usually lower the blood pressure.

- *Body Temperature* - will usually be normal.

- *Lowered Respiration* - under 20 breaths per minute.

ROMBERG

A person under the influence of alcohol will have a distorted Romberg. In lower doses, alcohol acts as a stimulant, so the person would most likely perform a rapid Romberg. In higher doses, alcohol acts as a depressant; hence the user would display a delayed Romberg.

OTHER OBJECTIVE SYMPTOMS

- Euphoria
- Hyperactivity
- Sedation
- Slowed reactions
- Increased risk taking
- Impaired vision
- Poor coordination
- Gait ataxia
- Impaired divided attention
- Slurred speech
- Poor balance
- Impaired cognitive skills

- Poor judgment
- Poor decision making
- Lack of short term memory
- Delayed reactions

SIGNS OF INGESTION

The odor of alcohol can usually be detected on the breath and person.

DURATION OF EFFECTS

The body eliminates approximately 0.015% of the Blood Alcohol Concentration per hour. This is equivalent to about 2/3 bottles of a beer, a glass of wine, or a standard mixed drink.

WITHDRAWAL

Withdrawal from alcohol intoxication by persons who are biologically addicted can be severe and even fatal. Delirium tremens (DT's) are also common due to the depletion of dopamine and serotonin. These symptoms are characterized by:

- Dilated pupils
- Chills
- Nausea
- Sweating
- Tremors
- Deliriums
- Coma
- Death

<u>SUMMARY</u>

Horizontal Gaze Nystagmus	*Yes*
Vertical Gaze Nystagmus	*Yes*
Non–Convergence	*Yes*
Pupil Size	*Normal*
Pupillary Reaction to Light	*Slow*
Pulse Rate	*Up*
Blood Pressure	*Down*
Body Temperature	*Normal*
Muscle Tone	*Flaccid*
Romberg Exam	*Fast*

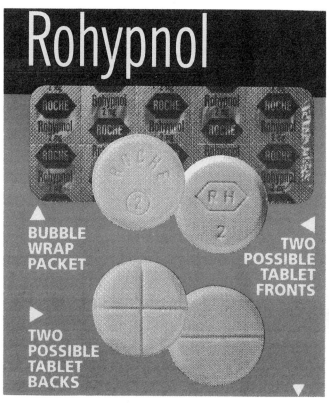

Rohypnol

ROHYPNOL

BACKGROUND

Rohypnol (flunitrazepam) is a prescription sleeping aid produced by Roche Laboratories. This drug is an anti-anxiety tranquilizer, and it is classified as a depressant. However, since the illicit use of Rohypnol has gained recent popularity, it will be separately addressed in this chapter.

Rohypnol is one of a widely used class of prescription medications known as benzodiazepines. It is primarily prescribed by physicians for short-term treatment of patients with severe and debilitating sleep disorders. This drug is not manufactured or sold in the United States, however, it is approved for use in 64 other countries. There have been reports that the drug is being illegally diverted, primarily from Mexico, and being illegally sold on our streets.

Rohypnol has become a popular drug of abuse in some circles. It has also been tagged as a date rape drug, for when dissolved in an alcoholic beverage, the victim may be rendered helpless and be sexually violated.

RECOGNITION

Rohypnol tables are white. They are stamped with the brand name "Roche" on one side along with an encircled numeral 1 or 2. A single cross score appears on the other side. The new one-milligram tablet is oval and green, which is more easily detected if covertly slipped into someone's drink. The tablet dissolves very slowly in liquid and releases a bright blue dye once it dissolves.

METHOD OF INJESTION

In tablet form, Rohypnol is taken orally. The tablets can also be crushed into a powder and snorted into the nose, or injected intravenously. Another common method is to dissolve the tablets in a beverage and drink it.

STREET SLANG

- Roachies
- La Roche
- Rope
- Rib Roche
- Roofies

- Ruffies
- Mexican Valium
- R-2
- Roach - 2
- Date Rape Drug

METHOD OF PACKAGING

The tablets are often illicitly sold in their original bubble-wrap pharmaceutical packaging. These are also referred to as blister wraps.

SYMPTOMATOLOGY

A person under the influence of Rohypnol will display symptoms of influence consistent with other Central Nervous System Depressants. This includes both horizontal and vertical nystagmus, and non-convergence. Vertical nystagmus and non-convergence would most likely be present in higher doses. Other symptoms include a lowered pulse rate, lowered blood pressure, a decreased respiratory rate, and a normal body temperature. The pupil size should not be affected, but they may be sluggish in response to the absence or presence of light.

When consumed with alcohol, a synergistic or additive depressant effect takes place. This may result in increased intoxication to the point of complete incapacitation with resulting amnesia. Depending on the dose taken, this synergistic effect could be fatal.

OTHER SYMPTOMS

- Drowsiness
- Dizziness
- Confusion
- Lessening of inhibitions
- Impaired motor skills
- Impaired judgment
- Coma
- Death

DURATION OF EFFECTS

Generally, sedative effects are felt within 20 to 30 minutes. Strongest effects occur within one to two hours, with overall sedative effects lasting six to eight hours following a two-milligram dose. The manufacturer, as a means of discouraging abuse, is now removing this two-milligram pill from the market.

SUMMARY

Horizontal Gaze Nystagmus	*Yes*
Vertical Gaze Nystagmus	*Yes*
Non-Convergence	*Yes*
Pupil Size	*Normal*
Pupillary Reaction to Light	*Slow*
Pulse Rate	*Down*
Blood Pressure	*Down*
Body Temperature	*Normal*
Muscle Tone	*Flaccid*
Romberg Exam	*Delayed*

GAMMA HYDROXY BUTYRATE (GHB)

BACKGROUND

GHB is similar to a compound that is naturally produced in the brain (Gamma Amino Butyric Acid). GHB was experimented with in Europe for a while as a possible anesthetic. For a period of time, GHB was marketed as a steroid enhancer, then as a fat burner. GHB was sold over the counter in health food stores under the name of Gamma Hydroxy Butyric Acid, but in 1990 the FDA banned it for human consumption. Although potentially fatal, GHB has become popular within the rave and dance club circles.

GHB is easily produced in clandestine laboratories. The two most common ingredients include Gamma Butyal Lactone (a legal commercial acid) and lye or sodium hydroxide. When mixed together they produce a head and become GHB (Barruel, 1998).

RECOGNITION

GHB can be found in a white powder or in a liquid form. When in liquid form the solution tends to be thick, similar in appearance to clear cooking oil. When in powdered form, the powder is very fine, similar to talcum powder.

METHOD OF INGESTION

GHB is taken orally, often mixed with juice, bottled water or any other type of liquid. The solution is usually poured into the bottle cap and swallowed.

STREET SLANG

- GHB
- G
- Water
- Salty Water
- Blue Nitro
- FX
- Serenity

METHODS OF PACKAGING

GHB in liquid form may be found in small glass or plastic vials, often sealed with a white cap. It can also be contained in water bottles, or any other type of beverage container.

Officers have also reported seizing GHB in the following containers:

- Bubble bottles (the typed used by children to blow soap bubbles)

- Eye droppers (the type used for bloodshot eyes)

- Small bottles of mouth wash

- Nasal spray bottles

- Small bottles of hair spray (pump style)

- Breath freshner drops

- Vanilla extract bottles

- Food coloring bottles

- Liqueur bottles

The Food and Drug Administration reports that companies are selling new varieties of GHB chemicals under the guise of dietary supplements, substances that are largely unregulated.

SYMPTOMATOLOGY

GHB is classified as a Depressant Drug (non-barbiturate), so symptoms of influence will be consistent with other Central

Nervous System Depressants. This includes the presence of horizontal gaze nystagmus, vertical nystagmus (in larger doses), and lack of convergence. GHB will lower the pulse, blood pressure, and respiration rate, yet the body temperature should remain normal. GHB should not affect the pupil size, however the pupil will be slow in reacting to light.

Users of GHB may feel a warm euphoric high, and some report having hallucinations similar to LSD, yet others become extremely ill and vomit. GHB also has strong anesthetic effects, causing extreme sedation. Because of this, it is frequently being used as a date rape drug.

OTHER SYMPTOMS

- Extreme nausea
- Loss of bowel control
- Vomiting
- Seizures
- Amnesia
- Coma
- Death

DURATION OF EFFECTS

The average dose or "shot" of GHB is one or two teaspoons, or a "bottle cap." The onset of effects will appear within ten to fifteen minutes and normally last three to four hours. Depending on the dose taken, the effects of GHB may last for up to twelve hours.

GHB is undetectable in the urine eight to twelve hours after use. This is why GHB is popular as a date rape drug for most victims do not report the assault within this time period due to incapacitation.

SUMMARY

Horizontal Gaze Nystagmus	*Yes*
Vertical Gaze Nystagmus	*Yes*
Non-Convergence	*Yes*
Pupil Size	*Normal*
Pupillary Reaction to Light	*Slow*
Pulse Rate	*Down*
Blood Pressure	*Down*
Body Temperature	*Normal*
Muscle Tone	*Flaccid*
Romberg Exam	*Delayed*

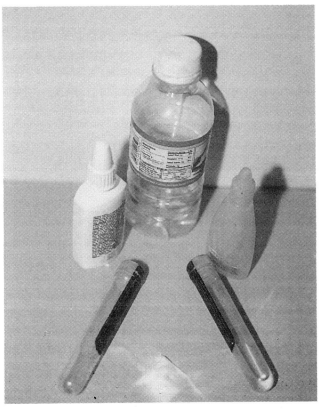

GHB

INHALANTS

BACKGROUND

Inhalants constitute a group of chemicals or compounds that when inhaled into the lungs can cause intoxication. There are three categories of inhalants; volatile solvents, aerosols, and anesthetic gases.

- *Volatile Solvents* - These include substances such as airplane glue, paints, petroleum products, cleaning fluids, correctional fluid, and nail polish remover. Many of these substances contain the ingredient toluene as the principal intoxicant.

- *Aerosols* - These are substances that are propelled from a pressurized container. The primary intoxicant is hydrocarbon gas, and include products such as deodorants, non-stick cooking lubricants, hair spray, and literally anything that is sprayed from a can.

- *Anesthetic Gases* - Most of these substances have legitimate medical uses in the management of pain. These gases include ether, chloroform, amyl nitrite, and butyl nitrite. Perhaps the most commonly abused of all anesthetic gases is nitrous oxide, commonly known as laughing gas. Nitrous oxide is often used as the propellant in whipping cream. It can also be obtained from some automotive stores for it is used as a fuel for racing cars.

RECOGNITION

Most of the items in this category are common household products and are of no violation to possess. Most anesthetic gases are contained in pressurized tanks and canisters, so they should be handled with extreme caution.

METHOD OF INGESTION

All of the compounds in this category are inhaled, or breathed into the lungs. Most of the *Volatile Solvents* are inhaled right out of the original container. The substance can also be poured into a bag or a sock which is held up to the face and inhaled.

Most *Aerosols* are inhaled right out of the container. Usually the can is held upside down to allow the gas to be discharged and to prevent the other contents from being expelled.

Anesthetic Gases can also be inhaled right out of the canister or container. Oftentimes the tanks are fitted with attachments which will allow the user to fill balloons with the gas. The balloons are then sold and the gas is inhaled out of the balloon.

STREET SLANG

- Huffing (inhaling)
- Whiffing (inhaling)
- Poppers (Amyl Nitrite)
- Locker Room (Amyl Nitrite)
- Rush (Amyl Nitrite)

SYMPTOMATOLOGY (OVERVIEW)

Persons who are under the influence of inhalants may appear drunk, disoriented, and stuporous. Because there are so many toxic compounds contained within these products, it is very difficult to predict what the actual effects will be from one substance to another.

Most of the *volatile solvents* that are inhaled (airplane glue and paint) contain the drug toluene. Toluene impairs both judgment and motor coordination.

The aerosols contain gases such as hydrocarbon which when inhaled, may cause pneumonia and damage to the larynx and the lungs.

Anesthetic gases such as chloroform and nitrous oxide can cause euphoria, hallucinations, vomiting, and unconsciousness. Drugs like amyl nitrite and or butyl nitrite cause a dilation of the blood vessels and can contribute to strokes and heart attacks.

In all cases, inhalant use is very destructive to the body, often resulting in organ damage, brain damage, and death.

EYES

- *Pupils* - Most of the inhalant drugs will not affect the size of the pupil with the exception of *anesthetic gases*, which may dilate the pupil.

- *Reaction to Light* - Regardless of the substance taken, the pupil will be slow and sluggish in response to light.

- *Nystagmus* - Most inhalants will cause vertical and horizontal nystagmus.

- *Non–Convergence* - Will usually be present.

- *Reddened Sclera* - The eyes will also usually be bloodshot, watery, and irritated.

CENTRAL NERVOUS SYSTEM STIMULATION OR DEPRESSION

- *Pulse* - When toxins are inhaled into the lungs, generally the pulse rate will increase. This is the case with all inhalants.

- *Blood Pressure* - Most of the inhalant substances will elevate the blood pressure. The exception is with anesthetic gases which will lower the blood pressure.

- *Body Temperature* - A person's body temperature may be up, down, or normal, depending on the substance taken. Most of the *volatile solvents* and *aerosols* will elevate the body temperature, whereas anesthetic gases will usually lower the body temperature.

ROMBERG EXAM

A person under the influence of inhalants will display a distorted Romberg which could be rapid or delayed, depending on the substance inhaled.

OTHER OBJECTIVE SYMPTOMS

- Euphoria
- Dream-like stupor
- Impaired judgment
- Impaired motor coordination
- Hallucinations
- Chemical odor on breath and person
- Product residue on the face and hands
- Nausea
- Respiratory ailments
- Amnesia
- Paralysis

DURATION OF EFFECTS

Persons can stay high on inhalants for 15 minutes to one hour. Most abusers will continue inhaling the substance until they reach the desired "high," or until the substance dissipates. Depending on the substance inhaled, the objective symptoms can be detected several hours after the last use.

WITHDRAWAL

Persons coming down from a high on inhalants often suffer severe headaches, nausea, paranoia, and depression. This condition may last for several days. Inhalant use does not cause biological addiction, but some users report experiencing a physical craving for the substance two to three times per week.

SUMMARY

Horizontal Gaze Nystagmus	*Yes*
Vertical Gaze Nystagmus	*Yes*
Non-Convergence	*Yes*
Pupil Size	*Normal or Dilated*
Pupillary Reaction to Light	*Slow*
Pulse Rate	*Up*
Blood Pressure	*Up or Down*
Body Temperature	*Up, Down, or Normal*
Muscle Tone	*Flaccid*
Romberg Exam	*Distorted*

Inhalants

ANABOLIC STEROIDS

BACKGROUND

Anabolic Steroids are synthetic compounds that act in many ways like the male growth hormone, testosterone. There are many legitimate medical uses for anabolic steroids including the treatment of anemia. Anabolic steroids have also been used to improve protein ingestion, inhibit tissue breakdown, promote muscle growth, increase calcium retention, enhance fat breakdown, and to treat skin irritations.

The illegal use of steroids to enhance athletic performance has been increasing at an alarming rate since the 1950's. An estimated two to three million abusers of anabolic steroids support a $100 million dollar annual sales market that is evenly divided between unscrupulous medical professionals, smugglers, and counterfeit clandestine laboratory operators (Miller 1992). Some athletes have used them in order to:

- Gain weight (10 to 25% within three to six months)
- Build muscle mass
- Increase speed
- Build strength
- Increase endurance
- Reduce recovery time
- Speed healing of injuries
- Increase aggressiveness

There is little debate that the use of anabolic steroids can make a person stronger, faster, and more aggressive. Yet, due to the associated moral, ethical, and medical issues, the use of steroids is prohibited in most athletic events and competitions worldwide. Additionally, major medical organizations condemn their use to enhance athletic performance or appearance (Tennant 1989).

RECOGNITION

Anabolic steroids come in two forms; liquid and pill. If the prescription label or trade name is still attached to the vial or ampule, it may be identified by the use of the Physician's Desk Reference. Some of the commonly abused steroids include:

- Dianabol
- Anavar
- Testolin
- Anabolin
- Winstrol
- Anadrol

METHOD OF USE

- Oral
- Injected
- Stacking - taking both orals and injectables

SOURCE

There are several sources for steroids. Much of the supply is diverted from legitimate medical sources, including the veterinary field. It is not uncommon for users to ingest steroids that were intended for the use on animals.

Very large supplies of illegal steroids are obtained from Mexico. In Mexico, most of the commonly abused brand names can be purchased over the counter without a prescription. The drugs are then smuggled across the border into the United States.

The illegal production of steroids in clandestine laboratories is also a growing problem, however, most of these labs produce bogus steroid preparations that are passed off as established trade name products. It is not uncommon to find ampules filled with vegetable oils with counterfeit labels attached (Kenney, 1996).

126

NEGATIVE SIDE EFFECTS

The abuse of steroids may cause many serious and dangerous side effects. Some steroid abusers exhibit uncontrolled fits of violence, anger, and aggression. These intense episodes are referred to as "Roid Rage." Some steroid abusers have reported that while taking large quantities of the drug, they are unable to control their temper, and any minor irritation can send them into this rage. Many steroid abusers have committed serious assaults and even homicides while under the influence of this drug. Hence, law enforcement personnel should use extreme caution in dealing with persons suspected of being steroid abusers. Other damaging side effects include:

- Acne
- Acromegaly (skeletal abnormalities)
- Elevated cholesterol levels
- Water retention
- Kidney damage
- Breast development in males
- Hair loss
- Growth of facial hair in women
- Deepening of the voice in women
- Swelling of the clitoris
- Shrinking of the testicles
- Impotence
- Lowered sperm count
- Irregular menstrual cycles
- Increased risk for cancers
- Strokes
- Heart disease
- Cardiac arrest
- Liver damage

REFERENCES

Barruel, Steve. 9/98. *GHB* (Unpublished Document).

Barton, Richard A. 1/96. *Ketamine: It's Not Just For Felines Anymore*. p.41-42. The California Narcotic Officer.

Blum, Lawrence. 1990. Police Psychologist. Santa Ana, CA. (Personal Interview).

Campoy, M.J. 7/97. *A Toadaly Awesome Case With Ribbeting Results*. p. 36-37. The California Narcotic Officer.

Kenney, Joe. *Anabolic Steroids*. 9/96. California Narcotic Officer's Association, 32 Annual Training institute.

Kilpatrik, Gregory. 8/93. *Nitrous*. p.36-37. The California Narcotic Officer.

Kilpatrik, Gregory. 1/94. *GHB Rave Fave*. P.36-37. The California Narcotic Officer.

McNeil, Don. 7/96. *Rohypnol: What's All the Fuss?* p.50. The California Narcotic Officer.

McNeil, Don., and Wells, Raymond. *The Issue of Miosis of the Eyes With Stimulants*. p.28. The California Narcotic Officer.

Miller, Gary J. 1992. *Drugs and the Law, Detection, Recognition, and Investigation*. Longwood, FL. Gould Publication, Inc.

Oglesby, Ted., Faber, Samuel., and Faber, Stuart. 1982. *Angel Dust, What Everyone Should Know About PCP*. Los Angeles, CA. Lega-Books.

Orange County Register. *"FDA Warns about Lethal Dangers of GHB Derivatives,"* May 12, 1999.

Radcliffe, Anthony., Rush, Peter., Scott, Carol., Cruse, Joe., Mende, Crystal. 1994. *The Pharmer's Almanac II.* Denver, CO. Mac Publishing.

Roche Laboratories. 1998. *Rohypnol Fact Sheet.*

Tennant, Forest. 1985. *Identifying the Cocaine User,* West Covina, CA. Veract Inc.

Tennant, Forest. 1985. *Identifying the Heroin User,* West Covina, CA. Veract Inc.

Tennant, Forest. 1991. *Identifying the PCP User,* West Covina, CA. Veract Inc.

Tennant, Forest. 1986. *Identifying the Marijuana User,* West Covina, CA. Veract Inc.

Tennant, Forest. 1989. *Anabolic Steroids,* West Covina, CA. Veract Inc.

Whitley, Ken. 1994. *Drug Identification and Symptom Manual.* Irvine, CA. National Consumer Publications.

U.S. Department of Transportation, Transportation Safety Institute, National Highway Traffic Safety Administration. 1993. *Drug Evaluation and Classification Training, The Drug Recognition Expert School.*

U.S. Department of Transportation, Transportation Safety Institute, National Highway Traffic Safety Administration. 1993. *Preliminary Training for Drug Evaluation and Classification, The Pre-School.*

KEY TERMS

ANALGESIC - A substance which creates insensibility to pain without loss of consciousness.

BIOLOGICAL ADDICTION - When brain cells must be artificially saturated with drugs to prevent the body from going into withdrawal.

BRUXISM - Grinding of the teeth.

CENTRAL NERVOUS SYSTEM - The part of the nervous system which consists of the brain and the spinal cord. It controls the sensory impulses and the functions of the body.

CHASING THE DRAGON - Smoking opium.

CREATININE PHOSPO KINASE (CPK) - A muscle enzyme which allows a person to exhibit super-human strength.

DELIRIUM TREMENS (DT'S) - Trembling and confusion induced by prolonged use of alcohol.

DIAPHORESIS - Sweating.

DIVIDED ATTENTION SYNDROME - A condition which limits a person from performing more than one task at a time.

DOPAMINE - A neurochemical which is closely related to the body's pleasure responses.

ENDORPHIN - A natural pain killer produced by the brain and the adrenal glands which helps control stress and maintain mental stability.

EUPHORIA - A feeling of well being and elation.

FLASHBACK - A repeated vision or experience of a previous occurrence.

HALLUCINATION - A perception of objects with no reality of existence, often caused by drug use.

HIPPUS - The pulsating of the pupil within a .5 millimeter range.

HYPERACTIVE REFLEXES - Jerking movements.

INTRAMUSCULAR INJECTION - An injection into the muscle tissue.

INTRAVENOUS INJECTION - An injection directly into the vein.

IRIS - The colored part of the eye which surrounds the pupil.

KILOGRAM (KILO) - 2.2 pounds.

LACRIMATION - Tearing.

MAO INHIBITORS - (MONO AMINE OXIDASE and MONO OXIDASE INHIBITORS) - These are antidepressants which metabolize serotonin, norepinephrine and dopamine. Two common MAO's are Nardil and Parnate.

MIOSIS - A constricted pupil.

MYDRIASIS - A dilated pupil.

NEGATIVE FEEDBACK - When the body stops producing the natural chemicals.

NEUROTRANSMITTER/NEUROCHEMICAL - Chemicals that are naturally produced in the body.

NODDING OFF - A condition of drowsiness where a person's head nods down and his/her eyelids appear heavy. This condition is associated with opiate influence.

NON-CONVERGENCE (STRABISMUS) - The inability of the eyes to cross or stay crossed.

NOREPINEPHRINE - A natural stimulant produced in the body.

NYSTAGMUS - The distinct jerky movement of the eyeball both vertically and horizontally.

OBJECTIVE SYMPTOMS - Indicators of drug influence.

OPIOID - A narcotic analgesic, also referred to as a narcotic.

PILOERECTION - This is commonly known as goose flesh, or when hair on the body stands on end.

PLASMA LIFE - The length of time a drug stays active in the body.

POST DRUG IMPAIRMENT SYNDROME - Brain damage caused by substance abuse.

PSYCHOACTIVE DRUGS - Drugs which exert an effect in the brain.

PUPIL - The dark hole in the center of the eye which is surrounded by the iris.

PUPIL RANGE - The range of constriction and dilation of the pupil, normally measured in millimeters.

REBOUND DILATION - In direct light a dilated pupil constricts then dilates back out in a pulsating fashion.

RECEPTOR SITES - Groups of cells that receive neurochemicals that send out messages to the body.

RETICULAR FORMATION - An organ in the brain which plays a critical role in the formulation of perception.

RHINORRHEA - Runny nose.

ROID RAGE - Uncontrolled fits of violence, anger, and aggression caused by abuse of steroids.

ROMBERG (RHOMBERG) EXAM - The internal time clock test.

SCLERA - The white of the eye.

SEROTONIN - A neurochemical which plays an important role in maintaining stable moods and emotions, and also helps regulate the sleep cycle.

SPEED BUMPS - Wounds and swollen tissue caused by methamphetamine injections.

STRABISMUS (NON-CONVERGENCE) - The inability of the eyes to cross and stay crossed.

SUBCUTANEOUS INJECTION - An injection under the skin, also referred to as "skin popping."

SYMPTOMATOLOGY - The science concerned with symptoms of diseases and drug use.

SYNESTHESIA - The crossing over of senses, seeing sounds or hearing colors.

TACHYCARDIA - Rapid pulse.

TATTOOING – Permanent dark markings under the skin caused by repeated unsanitary injections.

TOXICOLOGICAL EXAMINATION – A medical examination to determine the presence of poisons or drugs in the person's system.

TRACKS – Lines of scar tissue over the veins caused by repeated unsanitary injections which have traumatized the skin.

WITHDRAWAL – A condition caused when the blood no longer carries a drug to the brain of an addicted person.

INDEX

PHOTO INDEX

TOMMY DE LA ROSA
APPOINTED: 9-26-80
DIED: 6-21-90
KILLED BY DRUG DEALERS

IN GRATITUDE
ROTARY CLUBS OF FULLERTON